THE THAMES AND HUDSON MANUALS

GENERAL EDITOR: W. S. TAYLOR

Stoneware and Porcelain

D1232472

David Hamilton

The Thames and Hudson
Manual of Stoneware and Porcelain

with 115 illustrations in color and black and white

Thames and Hudson

Frontispiece Vase, 1960, by Bernard Leach (1887–1978)

© 1982   Thames and Hudson Ltd.,
London

First published in the USA in 1982 by
Thames and Hudson Inc., 500 Fifth
Avenue, New York, New York 10110
Library of Congress Catalog Card
Number 81-53054

Printed and bound in Hong Kong by
Imago with South China Printing Company

Contents

Appendices

Preface

This book is concerned with the art and craft of high fired ceramics. It is also an extension of some of the subjects described in the *Manual of Pottery and Ceramics* where the techniques for hand forming and decorating are discussed in greater detail along with the basic techniques of throwing and firing. This book can be read independently of that particular volume but it is important for the reader to realize that this one is intended for students who already have some experience and understanding of ceramics.

I do not concur with the opinion held in some quarters that stoneware and porcelain are in themselves more advanced subjects, but it is convenient to describe them together with the theoretical side of the science of ceramics, which is usually of concern to those students with some knowledge of the medium who have thereby experienced reactions, either exciting or disappointing, explicable only by understanding some aspects of the science of materials. Some students will prefer to ignore these subjects and remain dependent upon suppliers of ready-made ceramic materials who provide an excellent service for students and professionals alike, but within limits defined by the need to remain profitable. In my working life I have seen many materials previously available disappear from the catalogues and corresponding growth in the volume of ready-prepared materials. This must result in a reduction in the variety of ceramic qualities, and the purpose of increasing students' understanding of the science of ceramics is to release them from a dependence upon the most popular and therefore commercially viable materials and effects.

I would like to thank the staff and students of the Royal College of Art, past and present, for their assistance whilst I was preparing the material for this book, Graham Clark in particular, for allowing me to use some of his photographs of the mould-making process, and Mike Dodd for his generosity and patience in allowing me to photograph him throwing. I would also like to thank Studio House Rosenthal Ltd for granting permission to use a transparency of their porcelain cup, *Century*, reproduced on page 120.

D.H.

Introduction

High fired vitrified ceramics originated in China, Siam and Korea during the Shang Period (10th−3rd century BC) where naturally occurring minerals were found, allowing potters to develop kiln structures and clay bodies suitable for the production of stoneware and porcelain. It is unlikely that this was a rapid change arising from dramatic discoveries; more probably it was a gradual development through increasing firing temperatures and refinements of techniques for shaping, decorating and glazing. Some deposits of china clay or kaolin that are plastic enough to be formed and fired to produce porcelain without modification or addition are known to exist in China and Japan. The search for a refined stoneware or porcelain there was motivated not so much by a desire to achieve a translucent body as by an aesthetic quest for a cold and hard material like jade with a ringing tone when struck similar to that of bronze. This is the reason why so many celadons in various shades of cold colours can be seen in collections of Chinese, Korean and Japanese ceramics.

The art of high fired ceramics is believed to have spread to Japan via Korea during the fifth century BC but porcelain was not produced in Europe until the seventeenth century.

Porcelain formed part of the trade between China and the rest of the known world, particularly the Near East (Persia and Syria), and was carried together with silk from China overland via what became known as the 'silk trade route'. Gradually some of these wares found their way into Europe. The term porcelain is presumed to derive from the Italian *porcella*−small white and translucent sea shell−and to have been introduced by Marco Polo who visited China in the late thirteenth century.

The rarity and refinement of porcelain gave it great value. Not unnaturally there were many attempts to reproduce these high fired wares in the Near East and Europe, but they met with little success. Without the ability to analyze the original material from which Chinese porcelain was made, it would have required a good deal of luck for a Persian or European potter to come across a good quality kaolin as a natural deposit and recognize it for what it was. We now know that kaolins exist within those areas where porcelain was attempted. It was simply not found, or if it was, not recognized at that stage. A soft paste porcelain known as Medici porcelain, however, was produced briefly in Italy around 1580.

By the late seventeenth century in Europe few principalities or kingdoms were without an alchemist seeking to transmute lead into gold and to discover a material from which porcelain could be made. Most of

2 Teapot in soft paste porcelain, Vincennes, *c.* 1750. Victoria and Albert Museum

them realized that the degree of vitrification in Chinese porcelain was similar to that of glass, and it could not have required such a great leap of imagination to perceive that something analagous to glass cullet would be a useful component in a recipe. In 1673 soft paste porcelain for which a glassy flux was used was being made in Rouen. Translucency, whiteness and a high ringing tone when struck were the qualities which European alchemists attempted to reproduce in fine stoneware and porcelain, since collectors did not place the same religious and aesthetic value on their jadelike characteristics.

European attempts to produce porcelain

The invention of the process by which hard paste or true porcelain is made is attributed to J. F. Böttger, a German chemist, who was working in Dresden in 1708 under the sponsorship of the Elector of Saxony, Augustus the Strong. He found a deposit of what we now know as kaolin and from this he was able to make a high fired porcelain, which was developed in Meissen near Dresden. In 1710 there was regular production of this type of ware and by 1720 the composition of the body and its finished characteristics were identical to those of Chinese porcelain.

Kaolin and feldspar had been found in France in 1768 and by the following year there were factories producing hard paste porcelain, in some cases alongside the production of soft paste, but more usually ousting the lower fired composition. Soft paste porcelain tends to have a

9

short maturing firing range. Underfired it is not translucent and overfired it deforms.

Bone ash was being used to replace the glass flux in soft paste porcelain in England in 1750. A patent had been taken out in 1749 for the Bow Factory and Josiah Spode perfected its use at his factory in Stoke-on-Trent around 1805. The product became known as bone china.

Josiah Wedgwood, the eighteenth-century English potter, conducted many experiments in refining the materials, compositions and techniques of ceramics. Included among these developments is jaspar ware which can be regarded as a porcelain although it is usually coloured which renders it opaque. It is composed of clay, kaolin and flint with 50 per cent barium sulphate. He also developed black basalt which is made of a plastic red clay with manganese oxide which colours and fluxes the body.

Parian ware

The manufacture of parian ware, an unglazed bisquit porcelain, was perfected by the company of Copeland and Garret, Stoke-on-Trent, in 1842, and was in general production by 1846. The name derives from the Greek island of Paros, renowned for the quality of the fine textured white marble quarried there. In the early nineteenth century a number of potteries were attempting to produce an unglazed porcelain suitable for the production of small statues, but none produced a material as refined and lustrous. There was considerable competition in England to develop the material and the firing system which was necessary to ensure vitrification without distortion or collapse; the most successful firm in this field was Mintons. Unglazed figures had been produced in European porcelain factories such as Sèvres but these were much more expensive to produce than those made from parian. In 1850 a form of parian was being made which did not depend on total vitrification of the body, but to achieve the silky finish it was vapour glazed and could withstand a second decorative firing. This type of parian was coarser grained than true parian and also cheaper, but when soiled, however, it was difficult to clean. Parian was sometimes coloured with relief decoration in a contrasting colour—*pâte-sur-pâte*.

Salt glazing

Salt glazed stoneware originated in the Rhineland during the late fourteenth century where a tradition of high fired earthenware evolved during the following century. Its use became widespread for all types of ware, including relief decorated tableware. Brown stoneware became known in England at the end of the seventeenth century and a patent for a salt glazing process was taken out by John Dwight of Fulham in 1693. With the development of white and cream lead glazed wares salt glazing came to be associated, in the nineteenth century at least, with cheap containers, bricks and particularly drain-pipes where its resistance to weathering and attack by chemicals made it an obvious choice for engineers responsible for the laying of water and sewer pipes in the rapidly evolving cities of Victorian times.

Wedgwood vase by John Flaxman (1755–1826). Victoria and Albert Museum

4 Salt-glazed stoneware figure, John Dwight's Fulham factory, early 18th century. Victoria and Albert Museum

5 Brown salt-glaze spirit flasks from Denby
pottery works, founded early 19th century

6 Grotesque face jug by
Martin Brothers (from
1873). Victoria and Albert
Museum

Sanitary stoneware is a development from white earthenware made by increasing the proportion of feldspar and firing to a higher temperature, thereby achieving a vitrified body.

With the growth of interest in handmade pottery salt glazing has become a favourite technique amongst potters who could build or have access to a salt glaze kiln. The fact that the glaze develops within the surface of the body allows detail modelling to remain unimpaired by a coating of glaze. This is one of the reasons why many salt glazed pots show a preponderance of modelling detail either in the form of relief sprigging or ribs and flutes, all of which are enhanced by the quality and deposition of the sodium in the firing.

During the salting process reduction of the atmosphere takes place within the kiln and this limits the palette of colour; warm browns, orange, blue, grey and white predominate with a glaze texture varying from the characteristic heavy orange peel to a smooth glassy surface.

The process of firing is subject to severe restraint by concern for the amount of hydrochloric acid given off in the form of vapour, which is highly toxic and corrosive. Health and safety regulations have become restrictive and in most localities the production of salt glazed ware is prohibited or subject to control to prevent the escape of toxic gases into the surrounding area.

There has been a move by production studio potters towards the use of soda ash instead of sodium chloride because the former will make a glaze which is similar in many respects to that produced by salt. There is no by-product from toxic gases and salt glazing as such may disappear except for specialist use. If an economic way of neutralizing the hydrochloric acid can be found salting may be reintroduced on a wide scale as it has much to recommend it, both to industry and studio potters.

It is clear that all developments originally depended upon the availability of materials and the gradual improvement of equipment and techniques for refining raw materials. It gradually became possible to identify and modify materials without having to rely solely upon their appearance and pragmatic trials. Similarly this analysis has revealed materials which can be used in ceramics but which had not been part of the traditional ceramic range.

The development of kilns for high firing ceramics was not copied like the style or appearance of ware. But the reawakening of interest in the crafts has encouraged international kiln design with the introduction of oriental types into Europe and America.

Glazes, colours and decorative techniques are aspects of style as well as technique. They must match the firing temperatures of the body although on-glaze colours that were developed in China to decorate white porcelain were also applied to earthenware with little or no alteration.

1   High temperature kilns

Kilns suitable for high temperature firing must use large quantities of fuel or be very efficient in extracting energy from smaller quantities and transmitting that energy to the ware.

The method of extracting maximum energy depends upon the type of fuel. The initial burning of oil and gas requires large quantities of oxygen and to ensure efficient combustion a supply of secondary air must be introduced beyond the burner in the area of the flame. Some energy is lost because the flame has to heat up this secondary air, and efficiency is improved if this air can be preheated by drawing it into the kiln through a passage which is warmed by the firing process.

Burners and fuels

Gas burners: there are two types. The simplest is the atmospheric one which expels the gas into the burner port of the kiln. The system is shown in ill. 7. The gas enters the venturi, a device whereby a stream of one gas entrains another gas (in this case the second gas being air), through a jet which varies in size according to the type of gas, i.e. town (coal gas), natural or propane. The gas entrains air as it passes into the burner pipe and is ignited as it enters the kiln. The resultant flame commences 4 or 5 ins from the end of the pipe which remains relatively cool. Secondary air enters the systems through a specially designed port and ensures that there is an excess of oxygen in the kiln atmosphere so that all the fuel is completely burned. In this system it is the pressure of the gas and the speed with which it leaves the jet which determines the amount of air entrained.

The second one is the forced air type, where the air is supplied by a fan and the gas is entrained by the air. The air and gas are piped to the area where they mix, about 18 ins from the burner and the mixture of air and gas is fed into the kiln through an airtight system.

Forced air kilns require an exit flue for the hot gases, but the draught is established by the pressure of the fan and in most systems the height of the chimney is not critical to the effectiveness of the kiln.

Gas/air mixtures are explosive and must be treated cautiously. In order of calorific value propane is the highest, natural gas less and town gas lowest of all. The amount of gas required to heat a kiln of given volume to a given temperature varies in inverse proportion to the calorific value of gas used.

Atmospheric burners are regulated by controlling the flow of gas only, provided the venturi is not blocked to exclude air and the secondary air

Figure of Kuan-Yin, Goddess of Mercy, blanc-de-chine porcelain. Chinese, early 18th century. Height 15 ins. Salting Bequest, Victoria and Albert Museum ▷

port is left open. Forced air burners are controlled by regulating both the air and gas flows, but again the secondary air port should be left open.

Oil burners are of the forced air type. The air atomizes the liquid oil and the mixture is ignited as it leaves the burner. Further air may be entrained as the burning atomized oil enters the kiln but a secondary air supply is essential for efficient combustion.

Drip feed oil burners provide an alternative oil burning system in which oil is 'cracked' by mixing it with water. The flow of oil is regulated so that it drips on to a hot plate set within the kiln. The water is similarly regulated so that it mixes with the oil as it drips into the kiln. The heavy oil is decomposed to produce lighter hydrocarbons in the presence of the water vapour. The oil and water vapour will require primary and secondary air supplies. This burner must be preheated with a blow torch if necessary to make the plate hot enough to ignite the oil.

Solid fuels such as wood and coal burn in two identifiable stages: first there is a preliminary charring which releases some energy, but then much of the energy within the fuel is only released at far higher temperatures over more prolonged periods.

Solid fuel must be burned in a fire box (wood) or hearth (coal and coke). Fire boxes need to be rebuilt from time to time because of the great heat generated in this area, and must always be built of the hardest refractory. Fire bars which are used to hold coal as it burns must be replaced at more frequent intervals.

Fuels such as oil, wood, coal or bottled gas should be stored away from the heat given off by the kiln. Never leave an oil firing kiln unattended. If a leak should occur the oil may flood the area surrounding the kiln and suddenly ignite if fumes were to come into contact with a burner, so engulfing the kiln in flames.

A solid fuel kiln is best built outside the studio and roofed over to protect it from the elements and to make firing a little more comfortable. Large kilns may require more than thirty hours to complete a firing, with constant adjustment, stoking or regulating.

Kilns

Down draught kiln: this is the most efficient kind of open flame kiln and therefore one that will attain high temperatures in the most economical way. The flue which draws the gases out of the kiln is set in the floor and thus the natural tendency of the hot gases to rise to the top of the kiln is balanced by the need of the gases to find their way past the ware and out into the chimney. In this way, cool spots of heavier air fall into the bottom of the kiln where they are drawn away into the flue and the temperature within the kiln is more even than in other types of open flame kiln.

Electric kilns usually have a maximum operating temperature of 1300°C. Above this temperature the insulating structure of the kiln is less efficient and may even start to break down. Moreover, the elements within the kiln may melt if the temperature is increased much beyond this recommended maximum. With the growing use of ceramic fibre

◁ *The Clodion Venus.* Tinted parian, after Clodion. Made by Mintons, Stoke-on-Trent, 1873. Victoria and Albert Museum

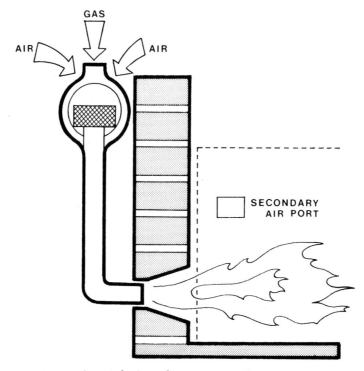

7 Atmospheric gas burner: section through the side of the kiln

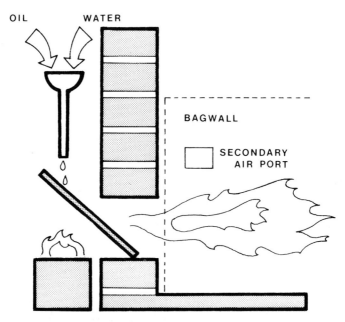

8 Drip feed oil burner: section through the side of the kiln. (The fire beneath the plate is used only until the burner is hot)

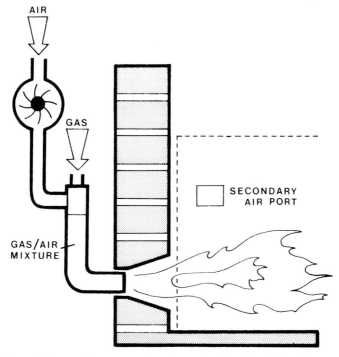

9 Forced air gas burner: section through the side of the kiln

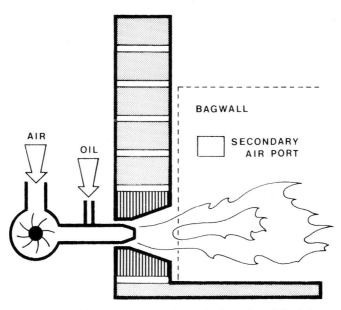

10 Forced air oil burner: section through the side of the kiln

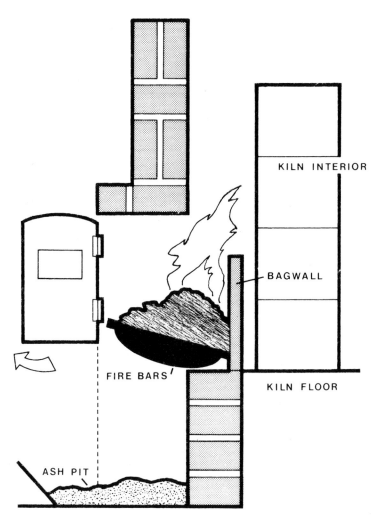

11 Coal burning hearth: section through the side of the kiln

insulation electric kilns have become far more efficient. Insulation bricks absorb much less heat than hard refractories, but far more than ceramic fibre. Therefore, ceramic fibre insulated kilns can have fewer elements per cubic foot and still achieve stoneware temperatures. If electricity is very expensive ceramic fibre kilns will be worth the slightly greater cost over brick built kilns. As electric kilns have no natural draught they must be well ventilated during the initial firing to ensure that water vapour and gases given off can escape easily from the ware and not creep out through gaps in the door. Water vapour is acidic and will corrode the metal casing.

Multi-chamber kilns make use of the exhaust hot gases from one chamber by drawing them into the adjacent chamber. The more chambers in the system the greater the efficiency.

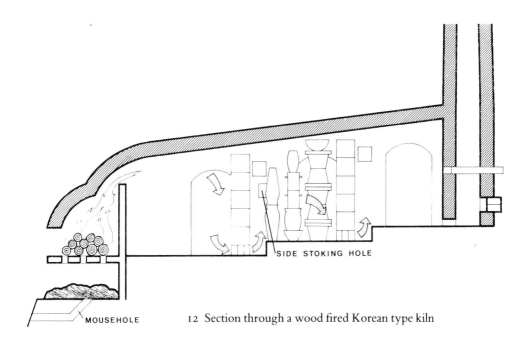

SIDE STOKING HOLE

MOUSEHOLE   12 Section through a wood fired Korean type kiln

Korean kilns are not divided into chambers. They consist of a continuous chamber with a firebox at the lower end. The kiln is set with pots and at intervals along its length saggars are used to construct walls across the width of the kiln. These serve as walls or baffles to divert the flames downwards where they travel into the next section by means of a chequered base. As the fire travels up the kiln, heat is given off and, in order to achieve the necessary temperature in each section, the firing is topped up by stoking it with wood through holes provided for this purpose (side stoking).

Natural draught kilns require tall chimneys to pull the exhaust gases from the kiln. In the early stages of firing the chimney is full of cold air which prevents the warm air from rising easily. Such kilns are built with a section of the chimney, say 1 ft sq. of loose bricks, which can be removed and a fire lit in the base of the chimney. In this way, the chimney is filled with warm air that rises and exits into the atmosphere so creating a draught in the kiln that draws the gases to the bottom of the kiln through the flue and into the chimney. Whilst this is happening, the removeable section of the chimney must be replaced so that cold air cannot enter the stack and reduce the efficiency of the draught. Under reduction conditions the easing or opening of this section to some degree will lessen the draught and aid the reduction firing. As unburnt gases are necessary to effect reduction in the kiln these gases will ignite in the presence of oxygen introduced as air into the chimney and flames may be observed in the chimney at this stage of the firing. Under normal or oxidizing conditions the flames should not extend into the lower chimney sections.

23

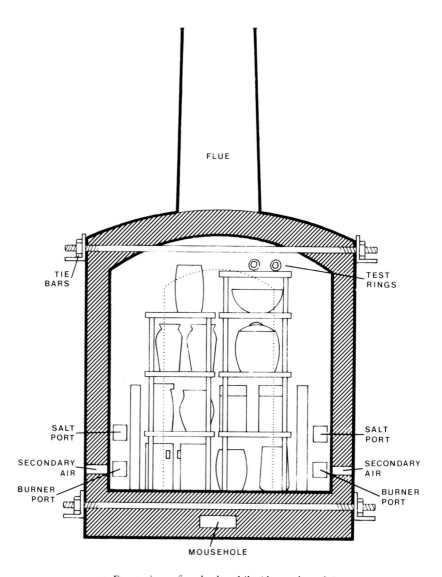

13 Front view of a salt glaze kiln (down draught)

Stoneware and porcelain firing kilns must be built of good refractory material. This can be for the most part insulating refractory, but where heat is to be transmitted within the kilns, i.e. bag walls, etc., they should be built of hard refractory. Fire boxes for oil, wood and coal firing must be lined with hard refractory to build up heat in this area and aid in maintaining ignition of the fuel.

The outside of the kiln should be of sound insulating material to reduce the amount of heat conducted through the fabric of the kiln and into the surrounding atmosphere. Such materials range from low grade insulation bricks (because the temperature to which they are subjected is not very great, say 600°C maximum) to mixtures of clay, sand, straw or sawdust smeared over the surface to a depth of 4 to 6 ins.

The size of kiln is dependent upon the amount of ware being made. It is not usually desirable to have unfinished ware stored in large quantities awaiting firing. It is also undesirable to fire every day and yet never manage to fire in one month the amount of ware that can be made in that time.

Salt glazing kilns must be of the open flame type so that the salt vapour can be carried with the hot gases produced by the burner to each pot being fired. Downdraught kilns ensure a more even flow of heat throughout the kiln and therefore a more even deposition of salt vapour than will an updraught kiln. As the salt melts any free silica which it touches it follows that all exposed bricks, props and shelving which form the interior structure, packing supports, fire boxes, flues and even the chimney, will be glazed by the action of the salt. Since the salt attacks the interior fabric of the kiln, it builds up deposits of glaze on the brickwork. When the interior is completely glazed much less salt is required to produce a satisfactory salt glaze finish on the pots.

A new kiln may require six or more salt glaze firings before the kiln itself is salt glazed sufficiently to produce a rich and consistent deposit of salt on the ware. With each firing the salt penetrates further and further into the bricks of which the interior is constructed until they decompose to the point where the fabric of the kiln is insecure. At this point the kiln must be relined or possibly completely rebuilt. To resist or delay this effect the fire boxes which are subjected to the heaviest salting must be constructed of either hard refractories or castable alumina which is not attacked by sodium. The lining of the kiln should be of hard refractory high alumina brick rather than soft insulating brick which decomposes rapidly with salt firings.

It has been found that once the initial salting of the kiln has produced a glaze upon the bricks the decomposition is slowed down and it may be possible that glazing the interior of the kiln with a transparent stoneware glaze will speed up the maturing of the kiln so fewer firings are needed before the acceptable level of glaze develops on the ware whilst simultaneously slowing down the decomposition of the kiln fabric. Some potters coat the interior of the kiln with alumina hydrate to resist salt attack and also to prevent any build up of glaze.

The design of the salt glazing kiln varies from that of a conventional stoneware kiln in the provision of salting ports above the burners. It is through these that the salt is thrown into the path of the flame.

The chimney should be lined with hard refractories to a height of 6 feet as the sodium gases escaping from the kiln are hot enough to decompose softer brick very rapidly. Above 6 feet this effect should be less of a problem since the gases cool as they pass up the chimney. It is inadvisable to use metal cylinders at any point in the construction of the chimney because the hydrochloric acid will corrode the metal as it escapes into the atmosphere. There should be provision for a refractory damper in the lower section of the chimney so that when closed it will hold the salt gases in the firing chamber.

It is necessary to pack a salt kiln more openly than a normal stoneware setting and the kiln should be designed to allow for this when deciding

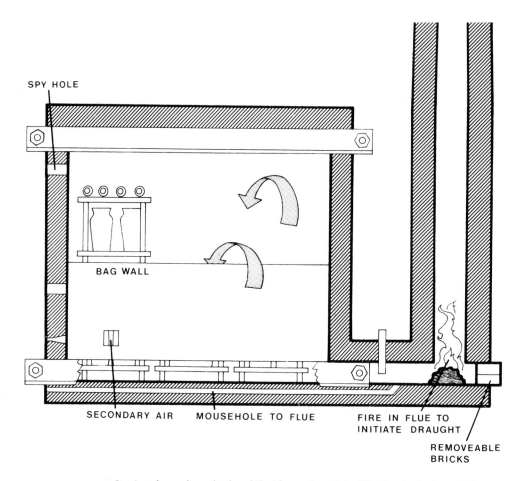

SPY HOLE

BAG WALL

SECONDARY AIR   MOUSEHOLE TO FLUE   FIRE IN FLUE TO
                                       INITIATE DRAUGHT

REMOVEABLE
BRICKS

14 Section through a salt glaze kiln (down draught). (The fire in the base of the
chimney is set only until the chimney is warm thereby inducing a draught)

upon the size of setting area required for a given quantity of ware.

Once a kiln has been fired with salt it is impossible to produce normal
stoneware glazes unaffected in some way by salt because any deposits
will volatilize when refired. For this reason studio potters may have
several kilns, one of which is used exclusively for salt glazed ware.

Salt glazing kilns must be built outdoors and well away from other
buildings. The chimney should be double the normal height, i.e. the
height of the chimney which would be built for a kiln of identical design
and using the same fuel (that which would produce an efficient draught
in a kiln), so that the toxic gases can be sent well up into the atmosphere.
To maintain the speed of gases as they pass up and out of the chimney the
upper third should be tapered to compensate for the contraction of the
gases as they cool.

All external iron work, tie bars, etc. must be painted with aluminium
paint to resist corrosion by the hydrochloric acid produced during firing.
Do not fire on heavy overcast or damp days as this sort of weather will
hold the fumes near the kiln.

Make sure no cars are parked nearby. If possible, design the kiln so that it has a run of 3 or 4 feet from the back of the kiln into the chimney stack. Set the damper in this flue and after each salting is complete, release the gases into the atmosphere by opening the damper and dilute the gases with air by removing one or two bricks from the base of the chimney. Adjust these to maintain adequate pull in the chimney, but the more air that can be added to the toxic gases, the more diluted they will be when they leave the chimney. An improvement on this design is to run a ventilating flue from the front of the kiln under the floor and into the base of the chimney, so that, when the flue is opened by removing a damper or brick from the front of the kiln, the air will run beneath the kiln and enter the chimney as warm air which will assist the rise of gases up the chimney as cooling inhibits this tendency.

2 The physics and chemistry of ceramic materials

In a brief description of the chemical and physical characteristics of materials, attention should be focused on those aspects which apply in general. The intention is to lay a foundation of understanding from which the reader can advance by referring to the *Further reading* list which gives titles dealing with the subject in more detail.

To comprehend the scientific principles of ceramics requires some patience, but perseverance is rewarding as it will help in conducting experiments and trials from a basis of knowledge so that progress may be made towards the desired result systematically rather than by chance.

Atomic structure

It is a scientific premise that all materials are composed of fundamental units called atoms. Each atom contains a nucleus of protons and neutrons around which electrons revolve in fixed orbits. The protons in the nucleus have a positive electric charge, the neutrons have no charge and the electrons are negatively charged. The electrons and protons are present in equal numbers, and as a result the electric charge in the atom is a balance of positive and negative charges. Neutrons are present in the nucleus in numbers equal to or slightly greater than the protons. Each atom can be identified in one of two ways: by its atomic number, i.e. the number of electrons in orbit around the nucleus, or its atomic weight, i.e. the weight of the electrons plus that of the protons and neutrons which make up the nucleus.

There are 104 different atomic structures known ranging from hydrogen with 1 electron to kurchatovium (the most recently discovered element) with 104 electrons which make up the 104 known elements, some of which are given Latin names and in chemistry are identified by the capital letter of the name, e.g. hydrogen H, oxygen O. Atomic lists are published and these are termed periodic tables.

The electrons revolve in fixed orbits with no more than 2 in the first, 8 in each of the second and third, 18 in the fourth and fifth and 36 in each of the sixth and seventh orbits. According to the structure of the atom not all orbits will be filled. Those atoms with 8 electrons, i.e. oxygen atoms, have 2 electrons in the first orbit and 6 in the second orbit leaving a shortfall of 2. Atoms with an incomplete outer orbit are unstable, and will try to associate with atoms of different structure so that they can acquire sufficient electrons to fill the outer orbit. This process is called ionic exchange. When atoms have changed their structure to achieve stability they are no longer referred to as elements, but as ions of that

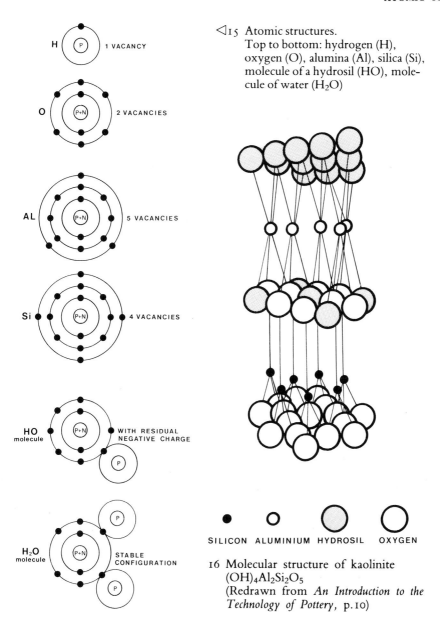

◁15 Atomic structures.
Top to bottom: hydrogen (H), oxygen (O), alumina (Al), silica (Si), molecule of a hydrosil (HO), molecule of water (H_2O)

H | P | 1 VACANCY

O | P+N | 2 VACANCIES

AL | P+N | 5 VACANCIES

Si | P+N | 4 VACANCIES

HO molecule | P+N | WITH RESIDUAL NEGATIVE CHARGE | P

H_2O molecule | P+N | STABLE CONFIGURATION | P | P

SILICON   ALUMINIUM   HYDROSIL   OXYGEN

16 Molecular structure of kaolinite $(OH)_4Al_2Si_2O_5$
(Redrawn from *An Introduction to the Technology of Pottery*, p.10)

element. According to whether the atom has acquired electrons or given them up the atom will have a different electric charge. They will have become negatively charged anions if they have acquired electrons, or positively charged cations if they have given up electrons. As opposite electric charges attract each other ionic exchanges bond together the participating atoms.

If atoms share an electron rather than giving it up or acquiring it, the bond is called a covalent bond which is even stronger than the ionic bond.

Ionic bonds produce brittle structures and covalent bonds produce hard structures: both have medium to high melting points.

In a periodic table listing all elements in order of atomic number, the first twenty elements include most of those regularly used in ceramics. It may be noticed that the elements in each vertical column have similar properties. The right hand column is made up of inert or noble gases and they have a completely filled outer orbit of their atoms. Each element in each vertical column contains the same number of electrons in its outer orbit and they will all combine with other elements in certain characteristic systems.

Periodic table

Group	I	II													III	IV	V	VI	VII	0
1st Period		1 H																		2 He
2nd Period	3 Li	4 Be													5 B	6 C	7 N	8 O	9 F	10 Ne
3rd Period	11 Na	12 Mg													13 Al	14 Si	15 P	16 S	17 Cl	18 Ar
4th Period	19 K	20 Ca	21 Sc	22 Ti	23 V	24 Cr	25 Mn	26 Fe	27 Co	28 Ni	29 Cu	30 Zn			31 Ga	32 Ge	33 As	34 Se	35 Br	36 Kr

The valency of an element is the number of possible links one atom can make with another. Hydrogen with 1 electron and 1 vacancy is monovalent and oxygen which is seeking 2 more electrons to complete its outer orbit is divalent. When hydrogen and oxygen combine, the oxygen atoms require 2 electrons from the hydrogen, so 2 atoms of hydrogen must be available to satisfy this requirement: hence the chemical formula H_2O which is water. Magnesium has 2 electrons in its outer orbit and will combine with oxygen to form MgO because they are both divalent.

The atomic structure of each element determines the chemical and physical characteristics of the compounds which it can form.

As the electrons revolve in orbit around the nucleus the atom can be regarded as a sphere. A structure of more than one atom of one or more elements is called a molecule and will have a specific shape according to the packing together of spherical atoms as well as their number. If more than one molecule is formed the result is a molecular compound and may be made of atoms of a single element or bonded together atoms of several elements. A molecule is the smallest number of atoms necessary to preserve the chemical identity of the bonded atoms.

As each atom has an atomic weight so each molecule has a molecular weight. The way atoms bond together determines the chemical and physical nature of the materials on earth. Gases, liquids and solids are all made up of atomic structures. When a solid is heated sufficiently it will first melt to a liquid state and then evaporate as it boils. Conversely, a gas will become a liquid if cooled sufficiently and the liquid will become solid or frozen if cooled still further.

Crystalline materials

As the packing characteristics of spherical atoms together with the various types of bonds allow the formation of different molecular compound solids, so they give to each compound solid a specific shape and this is responsible for the crystalline structure we see in many materials including alumino silicates which are clays. Theoretically at least, one would expect to find a similar atomic or molecular structure no matter which part of a pure compound solid was examined.

It is known that clay particles are flat discs, the shape being due to their atomic and molecular structure which is such that the horizontal bonds are very strong, but the compound tends to shear or break at the point where the pattern of bonding starts to repeat. The structure of the clay platelet is made up of layers of alumina, silica and hydrosils. A hydrosil is an atom of oxygen to which an atom of hydrogen has attached itself to give HO, with an electron vacancy in the outer orbit of the oxygen atom. The bonds between the alumina, silica and hydrosil are very strong, but at the top and bottom of the molecule all the atoms have become stable and there is no residual electric charge to bond the next platelet to the first.

The more electrons revolving around a nucleus the larger will be the atom; therefore hydrogen atoms are very small and lead atoms are very large. When an atom shares or gives up an electron it becomes smaller because it may have lost a complete orbit, but also because the remaining electrons are pulled further inwards by the positive charge of the nucleus. Small atoms will pack between larger atoms and can sit in the holes left between close packed larger atoms.

As an atom accepts more electrons it increases in size. The increase in electrical charge of the atom permits the electrons to orbit at a greater distance from the nucleus.

Compounds such as clay minerals which have been subjected to decomposition through the action of water may have lost some of their soluble alkalies and these may be replaced with water in the form of hydrosils which are no larger than a single atom of oxygen. This accounts for the presence of chemically combined water, alternatively known as the water of crystallization which is present in the theoretical formula of clay, $Al_2O_32SiO_22H_2O$, which should more properly be written $(OH)_4Al_2Si_2O_5$. This chemically combined water must be distinguished from physically combined water or environmental water which varies in amount according to the wetness or dryness of the site from which the clay is removed. Chemically combined water is a permanent feature of clay and is dissociated only at temperatures in excess of 300°C.

Glasses

Glasses of which glazes are an example are fundamentally different from solids in that their structure is random in the same way that the atomic structure of a liquid is random, so glasses are sometimes referred to as super cooled liquids. If a glass or glaze is cooled very slowly crystals of a regular atomic structure might form (a process called devitrification) if the atoms have time to form regular ionic bonds. Without a regular

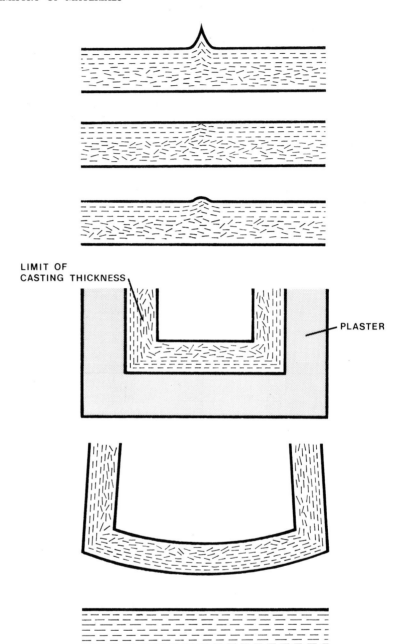

17 Particle orientation in slip casting
Top to bottom:
Section through casting showing clay running into a mould seam
The same section showing the casting after fettling
The same section after firing
Section through a plaster mould and casting
Warpage of a casting due to particle orientation variations
Classic card stacking pattern in a clay layer

structure to observe we must turn to chemical analysis to differentiate between one glass and another (Chapter 10).

Particle orientation of clays

The following remarks apply to all clays including hard and soft paste porcelain, bone china and parian bodies. All clays are made of plate shaped particles and their characteristic plasticity is attributed to the ability of the platelets to slide against each other when lubricated by a layer of water. The phenomenon known as 'clay memory', i.e. the reappearance of an early shape or defect in a finished clay form, is due at least in part to the orientation of the clay particles whilst the clay is soft and plastic. A slab rolled out flat and then curved and fired will tend to uncurl during firing while a thrown pot pressed to produce flat sides tends to become curved during firing. The illustrations show the particle orientation as a result of the initial forming and the later deforming of the clay.

When all the particles are so orientated that they are parallel to each other and are plastic formed, i.e. they are lubricated by water, the drying shrinkage is greater through the thickness of the clay than it is along its length because the water occupies a large proportion of the thickness of the clay. A cube of clay in which all the particles are horizontally orientated will shrink more from top to bottom than it will from side to side as it dries.

Whilst this is an important consideration in all techniques of forming clays, it can be critical when using clays made up of fine particles.

The drying shrinkage mentioned above is echoed in the shrinkage that occurs when the chemically combined water is driven from the clay crystals during firing (300°–600°C), and with fine particle sized clays, such as hard or soft porcelains, bone china, etc., these characteristics are more evident because the particles are greater in number for any particular thickness of clay and the layers of water more numerous.

When casting, particularly with deflocculated clays, the particle orientation will be parallel to the surface of deposition. Those on the base will be at right angles to those on the vertical surfaces, so that if the junction between the wall and base is a right angle the particles will echo the sharp change in direction and a point of stress will result because very few particles if any will lie in the corner and it will be formed only by an edge to edge contact.

Thrown pots show a similar pattern of particle orientation because the particles lie at 90° to the direction of the force applied to form the pot: thus all pottery displays more dimensional stability if it is built of gently curving changes in form, and this is why wedging is an important preparation to plastic forming. A random orientation is dimensionally more stable than a layered or laminated one.

3 Clays for stoneware bodies

Some natural deposits of clay will withstand temperatures in excess of 1280°C; they are low in fluxes and high in alumina and silica. Most include some iron and other impurities which will produce a buff or tan colour when the clay is fired. Commercial preparation of these clays includes the removal of some or all of these impurities.

Most potters work not with a naturally occurring stoneware clay, but with bodies formulated to produce the desired qualities in the fired clay. There are commercial suppliers of clays and bodies formulated to provide the most popular qualities including clays identical to those used by some of the best known potters. It is necessary to decide whether to use one or more of these ready-made bodies or to formulate one's own. The advantage of using a prepared body is that it will, or should, fire to the temperature indicated in the supplier's catalogue or technical data sheet. It will produce a colour and texture described by the supplier and it requires little effort to prepare for use. In baking terms it is rather like using a ready-made cake mix: disaster can be avoided, but the formula meets the basic requirements of a large number of people and therefore often lacks character.

A prepared body can be modified in many ways to make it more original or to produce a particular quality. Two or more prepared bodies can be mixed, but if this is done the result must be tested before making a lot of ware. Remember to test on this mixture the glazes and firing technique that are to be used.

Sand may be added to change the texture of the clay as can grog of various grades; commercial body stains and/or metallic oxides can be added to modify the finished colour. A guide to the proportions of commercial stains which can be used safely is usually available from the supplier and one for the addition of metal oxides can be found in the author's book *Pottery and Ceramics*. It should be remembered that the higher the body is fired the fewer the oxides that can effectively be used as some will volatilize if fired too high, and the higher a body stained with oxides is fired, the more they will flux the body.

Eutectics can occur in bodies just as they can in glazes and although this rarely happens in practice, it can be the reason behind some unexpected effects of combining bodies and colours (see page 115).

As reduction firing will increase the fluxing activity of iron, it must be allowed for when using mixes of iron bearing clay or adding iron oxide to a body.

If you decide to formulate your own stoneware body the range of materials which can be used and their function in the composition of the finished result should be understood.

Stoneware dish by Tatsuzō
Shimaoko, 1976

Stoneware pot by Hans Coper,
c. 1971

Stoneware painted pot by
Elizabeth Fritch, c.1975

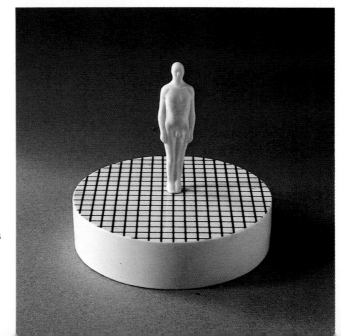

Bone china figure by Glenys
Barton, 1979

1   *Stoneware clay*: a natural mineral of decomposed felspathic rock. It varies in composition and working characteristics but should withstand firing to 1200°C. As a secondary clay it should be fairly plastic and include a large proportion of medium size particles.

2   *Fire clay*: a refractory clay capable of withstanding temperatures in excess of 1300°C. These are secondary clays which are low in fluxes and therefore plastic; some kinds are highly so. They are often found in association with deposits of coal and may have a high proportion of coarse particles which reduces the plasticity.

3   *Ball clay*: a secondary clay, highly plastic due to the small size of the particles with a high shrinkage during drying and firing. In a natural state the clay may be blue/grey or black due to organic material, but will fire to a white or cream colour.

4   *China clay*: a primary clay, produced by the hydrothermal decomposition of kaolinite and remaining on the site of this decomposition. It fires white, is refractory and shrinks less than ball clay during drying and firing.

5   *Kaolin*: very similar to china clay, but sometimes fires a warmer colour because of impurities present due to a different type of decomposition.

6   *Cornish stone* (*china stone*): partially decomposed granite. It contains feldspar, mica and quartz, and is fusible at stoneware temperatures. The purple colour is due to the presence of fluorspar. The darker the colour the higher the proportion of fluorspar and the more active it will be as a flux.

7   *Feldspar*: a naturally occurring mineral high in alkaline material in combination with alumina and quartz. A material of varying formulation which will melt at stoneware temperatures.

8   *Flint or quartz*: source of silica. Quartz is a naturally occurring granular form. Flint is obtained by calcining and crushing nodules of silica found in deposits of chalk.

9   *Whiting*: finely ground cretaceous chalk, $CaCO_3$.

10   *Grog*: the term applied to a clay or body which has been fired and crushed. It can be added into the plastic body. It is graded according to the particle size, e.g. 30s to 60s indicates that all the grog has passed through a 30s mesh sieve, but is retained in a 60s sieve. Grog is available commercially in many grades, but if it is to take on the same colour and physical characteristics as the rest of the pot, it is best to use grog which is made from the body of which the pot is made. Any pots which are damaged in the bisquit firing can be crushed or ball milled and graded by sieving. Do not use glazed pots as a source of grog unless the trials indicate that the glaze present does not excessively flux the body of the pot or produce an undesirable colour. Grog reduces the drying and early

firing shrinkage in a clay, but will shrink due to consolidation if fired to maturation after being added to the body of the pot.

11 *Bentonite*: a secondary clay of the montmorillonite type, very highly plastic.

Stoneware bodies are mixtures of clays, either stoneware clays, fire clays or ball clays modified by addition of feldspar or Cornish stone to make the mixture flux, quartz or flint to open the clay and make it whiter, china clay or kaolin to reduce shrinkage and plasticity and increase whiteness and refractoriness.

The above outline potential compositions which can be varied according to the temperature to which the clay will be fired, the working properties needed and the finish desired. As sources of clay vary so does its composition, and experiment is essential even when starting from a published recipe if the sources are not those of the originator of the recipe.

Fine stoneware bodies are most suitable for small pots and coarse bodies are suitable for large pots. Stoneware clays for jolleying do not require the same degree of plasticity as clay for throwing or hand building, and for slip casting should be formulated to produce the working characteristic described on page 93.

Stoneware bodies

	I	2	3	4	5	6	7
China clay (kaolin)	60	40	80	48	72		25
Fire clay		20	20	24		20	25
Ball clay	20	20		14	12	30	30
Feldspar	10			5	6	30	10
Quartz or sand				9	10	20	
Flint	10	10					10
Grog		10					

Modifications to a clay body

1 To increase refractoriness—increase the proportion of china clay or the particle size of the body.
2 To reduce the shrinkage—fire to a lower temperature or add some prefired material such as refractory grog.
3 To open the body—add coarse grog or sand.
4 To produce a finer body—ball mill the body or use more finely ground materials.
5 To increase the vitrification—fire to a higher temperature or add more alkaline fluxes by increasing the proportions of feldspar or finely grind some of the body.
6 To increase the thermal expansion—add more quartz or coarse flint (an excess may cause dunting).

18 Temperature gradient kiln. The ten trials are set up on a large refractory tray
which is placed in the chamber behind the rectangular bung on the right. The
top temperature is set on the controllers on the left and the rearmost test piece
is fired to that temperature. When the kiln has reached this temperature the
other trials will have been fired to various temperatures up to 200° C below the
top temperature. The dial in the centre will indicate the temperature in the area
of each test piece in turn when rotated

7 To decrease the thermal expansion—increase the proportions of clay
and fusible materials (and in so doing reduce the proportion of free
crystalline silica in the body).

Salt glazing clays

Salt glazing is possible because sodium is an active flux and will act upon
free silica in the clay to form a sodium alumino silicate glaze. This is
possible only at a relatively high temperature because the salt will not
decompose below 1120°C, but is only really volatile above 1160°C. The
process naturally lends itself to stoneware type clays, particularly those
which have a high silica content.

The chemical formula given for the reaction is:

$$2NaCl + H_2O \rightarrow Heat \rightarrow 2HCl + Na_2O$$
$$\text{salt} \quad \text{water} \qquad \qquad \text{hydrochloric} \quad \text{sodium}$$
$$\text{acid}$$

$$Na_2O + Al_2O_3 + SiO_2 = Na_2OAl_2O_3SiO_2$$
$$\text{sodium alumina silica} \qquad \text{sodium aluminosilicate (salt glaze)}$$

and a temperature beyond 1160°C is required to bring about this
reaction. In practice the glaze produced at this temperature is rather thin
and if the firing is continued (salting at intervals from 1160°C upwards),
the clay body may become very soft as the reaction penetrates deeper and
deeper. For this reason salting is restricted to temperatures a little below
the vitrification of the body and continued at intervals until vitrification
without deformation is achieved. The deposit of glaze is monitored by
draw trials and reflection using a metal bar or rod.

It has been found that clays containing 60 per cent silica and 20 per cent alumina create optimum glaze response. The remaining 20 per cent is a mixture of ceramic materials and associated oxides which will vary from one clay to another. Iron tends to reject the sodium deposited upon the clay, so the lower the iron content of the clay the smoother and shinier the resultant glaze will be. Coarse clays, i.e. those containing grog, and those clays in which the silica is unevenly distributed, i.e. sanded clays, will coarsen the glaze texture.

Clays with excessive amounts of silica tend to crack on cooling due to the reversion of alpha quartz to beta quartz at 573°C and cristobalite reverting to alpha cristobalite at about 220°C.

Engobes

To ensure the development of satisfactory glaze qualities it is quite common for engobes to be applied over green ware. These engobes may be made up of equal parts of ball clay and china clay. Where the resulting proportion of silica to alumina is almost equal the finished glaze can be matt, but if the proportion of silica to alumina is higher, i.e. 4 or 5 to 3, the glaze will probably be shiny. I say probably because the amount of salt fed into the kiln is another factor which determines the shininess of the glaze. Engobes with a ratio of 5 : 3 silica to alumina tend to craze.

Porcelain clays may be used in a ratio 2 : 1 with china clay: the engobes lend themselves to being coloured with colouring oxides as there is very little iron naturally present.

Engobes may be made which include feldspar in equal proportions to either china clay or ball clay, or both.

Colours for salt glazing

During salting a reduction atmosphere is created in the kiln and long periods of oxidization may be necessary to achieve bright colours. One of the most commonly used is cobalt; from 0.25 per cent to 2 per cent will produce blues of various hues. Iron present in the form of red clay or as iron oxide added to the engobe to produce 1 to 3 per cent iron in the glaze (red clay may contain between 4 per cent and 8 per cent iron), will produce pale tan or orange colours through to brown or black with the larger percentage. Titanium will produce mottling and is usually added in the form of rutile 4 per cent or 5 per cent as it introduces iron as well as titanium into the engobe. Copper (in the form of copper sulphate) added to the salt will volatilize and pass over the pots in the kiln to produce red (reduced) and/or green (oxidized) glazes. It will also affect the colour of the interior lining of the kiln and some copper will be held there and affect subsequent firings. This may be overwhelming and small amounts of copper can be deposited at certain points in the setting to localize the colouring. Copper, in the form of oxide or small nuts and bolts in a refractory container, should be set near the pots to be affected.

Mixing colours will produce more subtle and varied responses. As the whole process of salt glazing is somewhat unpredictable a good deal of experimenting is required, which lends a sense of adventure to a very enjoyable (but sometimes disappointing) ceramic process.

As colours can be varied so can the quality of glaze by putting more than one type of engobe on a single pot.

4 Clays for porcelain bodies

Porcelain clays are not naturally occurring; they are composed of feldspar, silica, china clay and ball clay fired between 1350°C and 1400°C to produce a white translucent body. Semi-porcelain is composed of the same materials in different proportions; it lacks the brilliance of true porcelain, and is less hard, but less likely to distort during firing which is 1200−1280°C.

Both types of porcelain are usually low bisquit fired (1050°C) and high glaze fired, 1280° semi-porcelain, 1350°+ true or hard paste porcelain.

China clay in porcelain provides the refractory structure for the fired body, the feldspar melts the silica and together they form a glassy matrix which appears translucent. As the china clay is the only plastic material in the body and is itself not as plastic as a secondary clay, the resultant body is very short and difficult to work, causing less of a problem for casting, jolleying or pressing, but making throwing very difficult, requiring great skill and practice.

The fluxing which occurs during firing is almost sufficient to form a glass. The recipe for porcelain glazes is only slightly different from that of the body. Any impurities in the porcelain body will be absorbed into this glassy phase and show as coloured spots in the body. The transparency of the body exposes these discolorations and this is one reason why only the finest and purest china clays should be used. Some suppliers (e.g. English China Clays) market a type of china clay known as 'standard porcelain china clay'.

Porcelain may be fired in a reduction atmosphere to reduce the effect of iron impurities in the materials by converting the ferric oxide, Fe_2O_3 to ferrous oxide, FeO, which results in a cold green-grey colour rather than the warm cream colour produced in oxidized firing.

The formulation of porcelain bodies depends not only on achieving the desired fired characteristics, but also on maintaining adequate working properties. If translucency or whiteness were the sole criteria very few varieties of porcelain body would be used.

As already seen, of the basic materials, feldspar, china clay and quartz, only the china clay has any plasticity and even this is very limited, so ball clay or bentonite is usually added to produce a more plastic body. These materials in their natural state are not without impurities, although the amount and type of impurity will vary. To preserve whiteness only the purest forms of ball clay or bentonite should be used and as bentonite is significantly more plastic than ball clay, a smaller proportion is necessary to produce the same level of plasticity. A lower quantity of bentonite introduces a smaller proportion of impurity and may be preferred for this reason. Plasticizers are vital in hand-making as they have the effect of

19 Pot in electrical porcelain by Nicholas Homoky, 1977

increasing the green strength of the drying body, and may be added to bodies to be used as casting slips although in this case a smaller quantity should suffice.

In working with thicker slabs of porcelain for hand-building difficulty may be encountered in drying the slabs because the size of the particle within the body is small and the capillaries through which the water evaporates are very narrow. The drying characteristics of porcelain can be improved by adding coarse material, such as calcined china clay (molochite), to increase the size of the capillaries but as it is calcined at 1500°C+ it may not be integrated into the fired body. The larger the particle size, the more pronounced will be the evidence of the molochite addition. An alternative is to calcine some of the porcelain body, and crush and mill the resulting porcelain until it has been reduced to the required particle size. If bisquited pots which are unsuitable for further work are used the low temperature of the calcining (in this case the bisquit temperature) will allow the added calcined body to be fused into the raw body as the firing progresses beyond the temperature of calcination. The finished result may be a body in which the pre-fired addition is indiscernible from the rest of the body. If the particle size is large this effect will be reduced and additions will be visible in the fired pot. Where the calcined addition is taken up into the rest of the body during firing the shrinkage of the pieces will be greater than where the calcined material remains relatively unaffected.

When making small porcelain pots the addition of gum arabic to the body may improve the working characteristics without changing the composition of the body. This plasticizer will burn out during the early stages of firing and therefore not contribute to the strength of the piece during firing. The use of gum arabic as a plasticizer is normally restricted to bone china and will produce a foul smell if the body to which it is added is stored for more than a week.

Fresh made batches are almost inevitably short which is usually attributed to either a disordered particle orientation or a lack of bacterial growth in the clay. If it is stored some bacterial growth will develop and this improves plasticity. I have heard of potters who add yogurt (not the fruit variety) to fresh batches of porcelain to promote bacterial growth, but have not had to resort to this myself. Ageing can improve working properties to the extent that nothing else need be added.

All vegetable matter, gums, bacteria, will burn out without affecting the body providing that it is fired in a well ventilated kiln so that carbon deposits are not trapped in the body as it sinters, sealing the outer skin of the piece.

5 Bone china, soft paste porcelain and parian ware

Bone china: a standard recipe is 50 per cent calcined bone, 25 per cent china clay, and 25 per cent Cornish stone or feldspar. This is fired at 1240°C and is translucent when brought from the kiln. Unfortunately it softens and becomes so pyroplastic as it matures that it cannot retain its shape unless it is fired upon a refractory or unfired bone china setter or in powdered alumina. It has a brilliant whiteness when fired, which makes it an ideal body for under-glaze and on-glaze decoration.

The body is commercially available in a plastic state, but if experimentation with the formulation of the body is desired, calcined bone ash should be bought, and added to the clay and feldspar. Slight variations in composition may vary the maturing temperature of the body; in all cases the maturing range is very short and it is necessary to fire the ware not only by temperature and pyrometric cones, but also by draw trials to ensure the body is sufficiently matured.

Bone china can be pressed into plaster moulds, jolleyed or slip cast: the latter is the most common because the material has little natural plasticity and the addition of ball clays or bentonite for moulding or jolleying must produce some discolouring. All containers, tools and moulds to be used with bone china must be kept scrupulously clean. The body will show any coloured stains particularly iron, which may come from an iron-bearing clay in nearby use in the studio, or from metal tools which have rusted a little. When making up a casting slip, it will probably be found that the proportion of 1000 clay, 450 water, 3.3 sodium silicate, 140° Tw, will produce a casting slip of optimum characteristics. For details of making up a casting slip, see page 91.

The whiteness of bone china allows it to be coloured with body stain in a range of pastel colours which are unobtainable with most other clays.

Soft paste porcelain is similar to bone china except that a glass frit is used instead of calcined bone, and the result is close in quality to an opaque or devitrified glass. The firing temperature of soft paste porcelain can be as low as 1000°C with a glaze firing at 500°C, but the normal temperature range would be 1100°C with a 900°C glaze. The body is not very plastic, deforms if only slightly over-fired (or over too long a firing cycle) and may appear slightly green because of the inclusion of glass. Parian body recipes are similar to those for soft paste porcelain.

Semi-porcelain is closer to white stoneware than to true hard paste porcelain. The translucency depends very much upon the wall thickness

20 Porcelain bottles and boxes by Jane Osborn-Smith, 1977

of the piece, rather than being an inherent characteristic of the body. It is more plastic than bone china or soft paste porcelain because it includes a higher proportion of clay minerals, and may be less white because of the inclusion of impurities in these clay minerals. The firing temperature is in the range of 1240°-1300°C. Some white earthenware bodies can be fired within these temperatures without distortion to produce a vitrified translucent quality. Where whiteness is an important consideration, the purest white burning clay materials must be selected, although it may entail shopping around trying out various china clays (kaolins), ball clays and bentonites.

Electrical porcelain is not translucent and, of the clay body types mentioned in this section, is closest to fine white stoneware. The body is formulated to vitrify at between 1180°C and 1250°C and may include pitchers of sanitary china to open the body during drying, which will become integrated with it when fired.

All these bodies can reveal a particular problem when slip cast in piece moulds. The seams can appear in the finished piece no matter how careful one is to fettle these when the piece is taken from the mould. This is due to the orientation of the clay particles during casting. Normally, the platelets of clay orientate themselves parallel to the surface of the mould, but in the seams they tend to flow into the small gap between the two parts of the mould and are therefore at right angles to it. When fettled, the particles no longer project beyond the surface of the form, but when fired the body consolidates and some of the particles in the seam are left sticking out beyond the surface of the piece. This condition cannot be altogether avoided, but can be allieviated if the seam is lightly hammered in order to reorientate the particles in this area or if the piece is refettled after bisquiting before being fired to maturation. If the body is left until it has matured it is so hard that it is difficult if not impossible to remove the seam.

Alumina paper is an ideal material to fettle white bisquit as it will not discolour the surface of the pot.

Parian ware: parian is characterized by its similarity to fine marble and is capable of a refinement in modelling which is due to some extent to the high shrinkage rate (20 per cent). The formulation of parian bodies aims to produce a vitrified, translucent porcelain type finish. The finer the grain, the smoother the unglazed surface and the higher the quality.

The basic structure is provided by china clay, fluxed by feldspar or Cornish stone and a low temperature frit or bone china or flint glass. As the body is very short, ball clay or bentonite may be added. If a pure white finish is required the materials must be free of impurities such as iron, particularly in the feldspar where it takes the form of iron silicate. (Note that clays and bentonite may include some quantities of iron.) The finished colour may range from a rather grey white to a warm cream or pink, and the colour can be modified by the addition of colouring agents preferably of very fine particle size such as cobalt chloride or copper sulphate.

If the fired finish is unsatisfactory, i.e. not smooth enough, the body can be glazed with either a lead frit glaze thinly applied before firing or the ware may be fired in a sealed saggar, the interior of which has been liberally coated with lead in the form of raw lead or lead frit. During firing the lead will volatilize above 1150°C and some of it will be deposited upon the parian ware, resulting in a thin, vitrifying skin of imperceptible depth upon a body of greater resistance to slumping than a parian which produces a smooth surface due to vitrification of the body itself.

During firing fine parian will need to be propped up or placed upon specially made setters, which may be made of the parian body, so that they shrink at a rate and to a degree identical to that of the ware. When such setters are used they must be separated from the ware by a coating of bat wash or alumina to avoid the two from sticking as they vitrify. Setters can be avoided with some forms by setting them in alumina.

Recipes for parian

1	China clay	45	2	China clay	60
	Feldspar	45		Feldspar	35
	Bone china pitchers	10		Flint glass	5
	Bentonite	2			
	Fired to 1180°C			Fired to 1180°C	

3	China clay	40	4	China clay	35
	Feldspar	13		Feldspar	45
	Flint glass	2.5		Bone china pitchers	20
	Ball clay	4.5		Bentonite	2
	Cornish stone	40			
	Fired to 1100°C			Fired to 1180°C	

5 China clay   38
  Feldspar   38
  Quartz   24   plus 2% or 3% soda ash or 9% pearl ash

  Fired to 1200°C

Parian 1 is slightly yellow and if any specking occurs it may be overcome by ball milling the flint glass, in the case of parian bodies 2 and 3, 2 per cent gum arabic can be added to improve plasticity during working. The materials for fine parian mixtures should pass through a 120 sieve.

Very small quantities of colouring agent may be used;

0.2%	cobalt chloride	pale blue
0.05%	cobalt nitrate	pale blue
0.4%	copper sulphate in solution	pale grey/green
0.5%	iron sulphate	pale green
0.5%	nickel sulphate	grey yellow
3.0%	cobalt nitrate	dark blue, suitable as a background colour for *pâte-sur-pâte* decoration

6   Forming stoneware and porcelain by hand

The basic methods of hand forming as described in *Pottery and Ceramics* can be used in shaping hard and soft paste porcelain providing they have sufficient plasticity, but are not suitable for bone china, parian bodies and soft paste porcelains which include a high proportion of glass frits because they lack the necessary plastic materials.

The problems encountered in hand building in finely divided clay materials are largely attributable to those which arise from particle orientation and accompanying shrinkage differentials.

It is vital when handling white burning clays to ensure that all tools, surfaces and hands are clean. Any contamination by other clays or metal oxides will be revealed in the fired piece. Even light coloured clays will contain some impurities, usually iron which will show as either a warm tan stain or a dark spot in the surface of the fired porcelain.

Metal tools which rust tend to transfer small particles of iron to the clay and produce similar effects. Stainless steel modelling tools are available and it is sensible to obtain some for this purpose.

It is very difficult to avoid contamination in a small studio in which several types of clay are in use. Red clay is the worst culprit. Some porcelains are relatively tolerant and can if necessary be glazed with coloured glazes. Bone china shows every spot of contaminating material and if it is used to take advantage of the whiteness, the results must usually be discarded. Do not return used clay to a bag or bin of fresh clay: it should be kept in separate containers so that one can be sure of the purity of the batch of unused body.

At each and every stage of manufacture, the same rules of cleanliness apply. Drying ovens or shelves must be clean as must kiln furniture, setting sand and lumina if used.

Forming porcelain

Coiling with porcelain is possible, but the results can be very lumpy. When rolling out or extruding coils the particles orientate themselves around the circumference of the coil. When these are set one above the other the drying and firing shrinkage compacts the coils and they pull away from the joint which must be well secured with cross hatching and slip, and filled with extra clay if necessary to keep the coils together. Nevertheless, the finished piece tends to show the method by which the form has been constructed, i.e. coils. Burnishing helps to reduce this effect because it tends to reorientate the particles on the surface of the clay. It will have little effect upon the particle orientation within the clay coil, however, and the rings of the coils still tend to be revealed during firing.

Pinching and modelling can be used to form porcelain and stoneware. If the work is made from one piece of clay the problems of joints either weakening the form or showing in the finished piece are both avoided and variations in thickness caused by varying pressure applied during the forming process can produce soft and pleasing irregularities particularly when a translucent firing porcelain body is used. Naturally, this technique does not easily lend itself to very large shapes as it is difficult to handle a single mass of clay larger than the size of a clenched fist.

Forming stoneware

There is no real problem in hand forming stoneware clays providing that the final structure is sound, well joined and can support itself during drying and firing, also bearing in mind that at the high temperatures to which the clay will be fired, the clay will become pyroplastic and tend to flow which can produce a 'slumped' or distorted result. The coarser the material, the smaller will be the surface area exposed to the effect of the heat and the more refractory it will be. The general rule of increasing the proportion of coarse, fired material (i.e. grog) according to the thickness of the clay section should be borne in mind. Whatever type of stoneware clay is used to hand build, particular attention must be paid to joints between pieces of clay. They must be of identical or at least very similar moisture content so that they dry and shrink at similar rates and the joints must be well made, i.e. cross hatched, slipped and the clays well seated to exclude air pockets, which would be weak points in the joint. Whenever possible, set a coil of clay along the inside of any corners to help reinforce the joint; if this coil is modelled to produce an internal radius on the inside of the corner, it will transmit any stresses to the body of the clay pieces being joined which might otherwise focus on the corner.

In all cases of hand building any modelling or corrugations even if they occur only on one side (inside or outside) will help the form to keep its shape.

Most recipes for porcelain and particularly hard paste contain a large proportion of flint. This is free silica (i.e. not associated with alumina to form china clay or with soda/potassium and alumina to form feldspar) and should not be inhaled (see Appendix 9). When modelling or fettling this type of clay, it is essential to wear overalls and carry out the procedure in a fettling booth designed to draw the clay dust away from one. If this is impossible, a suitable dust mask designed to filter out the fine particles of free silica must be worn.

Refining

If the surface of a fine grained stoneware or porcelain is to be refined and smooth without the benefit of a glaze it may be burnished. The fired result may, however, still be rather rough when touched, due to the vitrification and particle orientation lowering the level of the surface and leaving some particles sticking up. This effect can be reduced by polishing the ware after bisquiting with alumina paper as it will not stain the clay: it is available in several grades and one should start with a medium coarse grade and finish with a fine grade to achieve the smoothest results.

Joining

When joining pieces of fine porcelain clay a satisfactory union can sometimes be achieved by using water instead of slip. The areas to be joined should be cross hatched as usual and painted with water. When the two pieces are joined they should be rubbed together until they feel tight, which has the effect of crumbling the clay body in the area of the join thus forming a slip/slurry within the join without an excess that might flow over the surface of the surrounding clay.

21 Clay modelling tools

7 Model and mould making

Model making refers to any process where a prototype is made with the intention of making a mould and editioning or mass producing the original design. The two conventional materials for model making related to ceramic production are clay and plaster of Paris. During the eighteenth century most models were made of clay and bisquited to produce a strong and detailed original, from which a mould would be made, either of clay (later to be fired to produce a porous bisquit) or of plaster. Plaster of Paris has gradually taken over as it can be worked in various states and over extended periods. Both materials have the distinct advantage of being homogenous — unlike wood which has a grain to limit the freedom of the modeller — and are relatively soft — unlike metal which is slow and difficult to shape.

Clay modelling

When clay is used as a modelling material, it must be kept damp throughout the process and when completed will require no further treatment for a plaster mould to be made from it. The clay being soft will release easily from the plaster, although it is usually destroyed in this process. Even though the soft clay will always release from the mould it should be remembered that the final cast has to come from the mould undamaged and divisions in the mould must be located to facilitate this. If the clay model is to be retained undamaged, it will probably be necessary to bisquit fire it, then to seal it with shellac or epoxy resin before proceeding to the mould making stage.

The clay that is used in modelling must be of a texture that will allow the required surface quality to be achieved. It is difficult if not impossible to shape a finely detailed model in a coarse textured clay. The specially designed model making material marketed under the trade name 'Plasticine' can be recommended. This is a clay base bound with oils which dry very slowly. Therefore the clay does not need to be kept damp, simply stored in an airtight container or wrapped in polythene. When the plasticine hardens it can be softened by warming, either in one's hands or in a very cool oven. It should be purchased from a dealer in art materials as it is very expensive if bought in small packets from toy shops, or stationers.

Plaster of Paris

Plaster of Paris is produced by calcining powdered gypsum rock at a temperature between 120°C and 140°C. To produce denser plaster, which is required for detailed modelling and jolley moulds, the gypsum is burned in an autoclave. Intermediate plasters are blends of these two types. The chemical formula for calcining gypsum to produce plaster is:

$$2CaSO_42H_2O \rightarrow 2CaSO_4H_2O$$
$$\text{gypsum} \qquad \text{plaster}$$

Variation in colour is due to impurities in the gypsum. When calcining is complete the plaster is put through a 70s mesh sieve.

When water is added to plaster, it rehydrates and in so doing, produces needle shaped crystals which bind together the particles. The amount of water required to produce this rehydration is far less than that required to produce a pourable slurry. The plaster must then be dried when casting is complete so that the excess water may evaporate to leave a porous mould.

Store plaster in a dry room where the temperature does not fall below 13°C (56°F).

Types of plaster

There are many different types of plaster of Paris produced commercially to meet the requirements of industry, the medical and dental professions, and artists. Most manufacturers will supply technical information regarding types of plaster either through a supplier or direct. They also have technical representatives who will answer queries and may visit one's studio if requested. In this way, they can see exactly what the requirements are. Do not be tempted to buy too large a quantity of plaster at any one time: it deteriorates with keeping. Storing plaster for more than three months should be avoided, and even within this period a gradual change in the setting and working characteristics of the material will be noticed. Under no circumstances should the plaster be allowed to take up water before one is ready to use it, so it should be transported and unloaded under cover, taking care that no droplets of water enter the plaster bags when it is being mixed. So that one's hands do not have to come into contact with the plaster plastic scoops of a size sufficient to minimize the number of times one has to dip into the bag should be used when making up say four pints of plaster.

Storage

Containers for mixing plaster should have a very smooth surface and in a ceramics studio it is sensible to use glazed jugs. As these have to be drained upside down from time to time it is worthwhile designing the jug so that the spout or snip does not rise higher than the edge of the jug, otherwise the snip tends to get damaged. Plaster will then set on the unglazed broken edge and can be very difficult to remove.

One reason for using ceramic jugs is to permit easy cleaning after each mix. Setting times will be affected if there is some old set plaster in the mix. The older the plaster the faster the setting time, and there is always the chance of the old plaster being taken up in the fresh mix as a hard lump, which may affect the modelling at a later stage. Before blending make sure that any plaster on the lip of the jug has been pushed into the

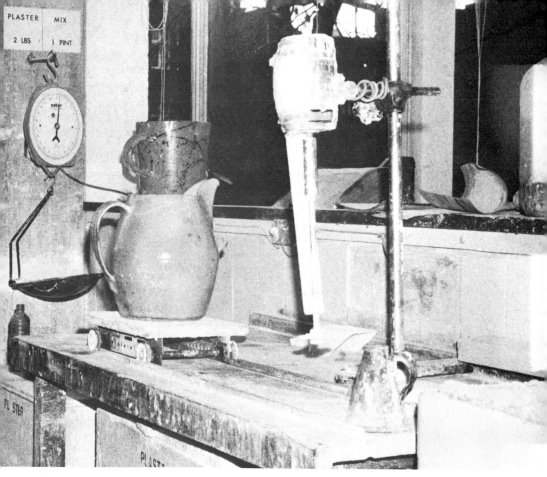

22 Plaster blending: scales, mixing jugs, variable speed blender, conical 1 pint measure

mix and the jug is clean so that no fresh plaster can drop into the blend at a later stage and upset the homogeneity of the mixture.

Mixing plaster

When mixing plaster, sprinkle it into the water to avoid including air in the mixture. Only make up as much plaster as can be poured before setting starts. Abide by the manufacturer's recommended plaster/water ratios, by weight, e.g. British gypsum potter's plaster 100/65 to 100/90, modelling plasters 100/55, crystacal 100/40. Generally, the lower the water ratio the greater the strength and surface hardness, the greater the resistance to wear, the lower the porosity, the less the setting expansion, the lower the drying time of the mould.

After the plaster has been sprinkled into the water, allow it to soak for two minutes to reduce the likelihood of lumps and encourage a uniform distribution of plaster during blending. Fast blending accelerates the setting time. Do not mix the plaster once it has begun to set. If the mixture is poured before it is properly blended, it will settle with an uneven density. If the mixture is poured late, the resulting mould will show layers which may separate whilst in use. This can happen when large quantities of plaster are mixed with the intention of pouring several moulds. When poured the plaster mould may be shaken gently to encourage air to rise to the top of the plaster mix.

As the plaster sets it gives off heat and swells 0.25 per cent potter's plaster, 0.20 per cent crystacal. At this stage in the process it takes up all the detail of the surface against which it is casting. When cool the cast can be removed with care. The compressive strength of plaster moulds varies from 2100 lb/in^2 (potter's plaster) to 4600 lb/in^2 (crystacal).

The more a plaster is blended the faster and harder it will set. Electric plaster blenders are designed to blend the plaster and water by a revolving impeller at the bottom of the mix, so the amount of air in the blend is minimized. In use, therefore, the jug of plaster and water is placed with the impeller in it before switching on and the blender is stopped before removing the jug. The impeller and shaft must be cleaned between each mix and this is done most easily before the plaster has set by placing it in a second jug containing water and switching on to remove some plaster. After removing the jug, the residue should be cleaned off the blender.

In some studios, it is the practice to mix plaster with warm water, but as the intention in this section is to describe techniques which standardize the qualities of the plaster blend, I think it better to use cold water because the temperature variation from day to day or season to season will be much smaller than the probably subjective decision of an unmeasured description of 'warm' water. The stated ideal water temperature is 12–18°C (54–65°F).

The manufacturer of the plaster will specify the optimum ratio of plaster to water for any particular plaster together with blending and setting times which should always be used unless experience shows that one of the characteristics of setting time or hardness can be improved by a measured change.

A good mould making or potter's plaster is, of course, essential to produce porous moulds for slip casting, a modelling or superfine plaster which sets harder than potter's plaster with a denser cast; and a brand of very dense plaster such as crystacal for delicate models and hard wearing jolley moulds.

There are commercial additives for plasters which will prolong or shorten the setting time and increase or decrease the hardness of the set plaster. Again consult the manufacturer of the plaster as proportions of the additives may vary from plaster to plaster.

Model making

This process in clay or plaster cannot readily be described as each job requires some degree of refinement or invention upon one or more of the basic techniques. These consist of either building up the clay or plaster or cutting it back. A clay model can be constructed by building up small pellets of clay all over the form and then smoothing them out with a rubber kidney or sponge. Alternatively, a mass of clay larger than that required for the finished form can be cut back with cutting wires, modelling tools or knives and then smoothed to the desired surface. Plaster models may be built up by casting a core and adding to this small amounts of liquid plaster either by pouring or throwing small amounts

23 Casting a mould using shellacked plaster blocks to define the outer edge of the mould

on to the core. A larger block of plaster can be cut back with saws, rifflers, files or surform blades. In both cases the finished surface can be achieved by working with finer files and then with sandpaper.

Hand tools for modelling clay and plaster can be purchased from suppliers of art and craft materials. They vary in price according to the complexity of their manufacture and the material from which they are made; e.g. flat wooden tools are cheaper than forged stainless steel. Each type has its use and the steel tools are difficult to make without quite sophisticated equipment. A variety of tools is required which will smooth, cut, scrape or file the modelling material. A personal collection can be built up over the years. See ills 21, 24.

Very precise forms and mechanical forms are probably best modelled using templates or some kind of regulating device. Organic models are usually best made by hand modelling. In all cases choosing the right technique for the job is probably as important as the skill in determining the quality of the final form and surface of the model.

When modelling clay one should aim to complete the model before the clay is dry. It is not a good idea to scrape or sandpaper the clay when dry as this generates a lot of harmful clay dust. It follows that most clay models should be simple and relatively quick to complete. It is, of course, possible to cast from the clay model into plaster when it can be refined with less haste.

24 Plaster modelling tools made of mild steel

Hand modelling of plaster allows great accuracy of design and detail. Handles, spouts and other more complex forms can be drawn out on the plaster using an indelible pencil and obviously the drawing must be accurate where the form being modelled is to fit another shape. In the case of a teapot spout which has a large surface area in contact with the teapot body, it should be cast against the body which has been soaped. The body should be marked with a centre line, one or two holes drilled into the body along this line, headless pins glued into these, and clay walls set in place to contain sufficient plaster for the desired shape of spout. A small amount of plaster is mixed and poured into the clay reservoir. When set, the spout is removed from the body of the teapot and trimmed to shape by cutting, scraping, filing and finishing with wet and dry paper. The spout can be tried on the teapot body using the pins to register and hold it. Several spout models may be made in this way until the design is perfected. It is not usual to make handles by casting them against the teapot body because the surface contact is normally not very great and can be modelled in the handle without much difficulty. When all the parts of the model are complete they may be joined to the body with glue if the mould is intended to cast the teapot in one piece. Alternatively, the spout and/or handle can be cast separately and luted to the clay teapot body before being bisquited.

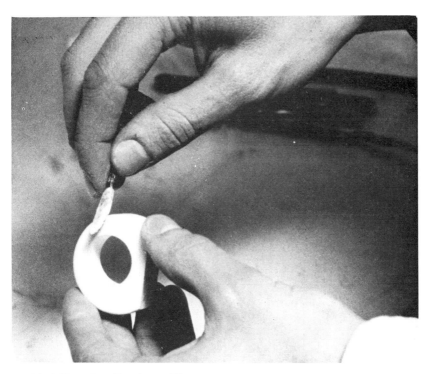

25 Modelling a handle using a riffler 1

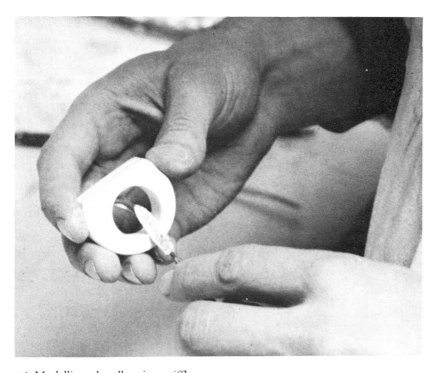

26 Modelling a handle using a riffler 2

Lids are not cast against the body of the pot if they are round, but are turned on a lathe or whirler and the fit ensured by careful measuring. Lids which are not round or those that lie off the vertical of the body and cannot be turned should be cast against a recess modelled into the body and then finished by hand.

Handles for cups, mugs and jugs are made in the same way as teapot handles. Spouts for jugs are modelled like teapot spouts. Beads or similar details should where possible be modelled by cutting a small metal template to be used as a blade. This must be done very carefully to ensure a regulated finish free from ripples or any other type of variation on what should be a smooth flowing linear form.

The novice will probably find that hand modelling is very slow and may have to repeat the work several times to achieve the desired quality of finish. Practice will speed up the process and this together with thought and care will lead to the skill and invention which are required in model making.

Lathe turning

Turning on the lathe can be done to produce unusual and decorative forms. Profile plates can be designed which revolve with the chuck and against which a tool holder can run. Travelling the tool along the length of the plaster will produce a prism with a plan identical to the original profile. If the plaster is shaped with a profile before turning with a tool, the resulting form can be very rich and complex. Turning is capable of infinite variation: some ideas will spring from incidents which occur whilst working with the lathe. It is best to have a variable speed lathe with a travelling tool holder, if possible on an automatic feed, to allow

27 Plaster blocks, plaster cottling and chucks upon which plaster is set before turning on a horizontal lathe

28 Plaster turning chisels

the use of cutting tools of various shapes and to pre-set the speed at which it travels along the length, as well as the speed at which it cuts into the plaster. A drop bed lathe allows one to turn shapes of larger radius than will a conventional bed.

This type of lathe is normally associated with engineering; many techniques spring from this field of precise mechanical work and the results can be very subtle and fascinating.

The plaster is cast on to the chuck or around the spindle and when it has started to set, but before it has become warm, the cottle is removed and the chuck or spindle is set upon the lathe and turning commenced. Woodworking chisels, paint scrapers, knives with large handles and small blades are used to cut away the plaster as it gets harder. Woodworking chisels may be ground down to whatever shape required. As the plaster sets hard the modelling will become slower and greater accuracy is possible. The model is finished with wet and dry paper which provides a smooth surface as well as moving a fine slurry of plaster over the surface of the model, filling in any pinholes in the plaster which are revealed as the modelling progresses.

29 Turning a plaster model on a lathe

30 Checking the diameter of a turned model using bow callipers

31 A small bandsaw for cutting plaster shapes

The model is removed from an open chuck by sawing through the stem holding it to the chuck or by turning the stem with a parting chisel, then snapping it off when the lathe has stopped. The model may be removed from a spindle by sliding it off the taper. When it has been removed from an open chuck, clean off the remaining plaster level with the chuck and then turn concentric rings approximately ½ in. deep to form a key for the next mix of plaster to be cast on to the chuck.

When work with the lathe is finished, all residual plaster should be cleaned off and the bed oiled. All tools should be kept clean during turning with the aid of a bowl of water and sponge. If the plaster is allowed to dry on the tools (especially rifflers), it will be difficult if not impossible to remove. Dry chisels and other tools should be dried and lightly oiled to inhibit corrosion before being put away.

32 A plaster model turned and cut most of the way through the plaster stem using a parting chisel. The model may now be sawn or snapped off

33 A plaster topped whirler with a shoulder rest which is pressed against the board suspended behind the whirler head

34 A plaster model turned in plaster on a whirler. Turning chisels, templates and callipers can be seen together with a sponge for soaping the model

Sledging

This is the term applied to the process of running plaster along a smooth surface and shaping it with a profile held in a frame called a plough or sledge. The surface against which the plaster is cast should be a heavy gauge, ⅜ in. at least, glass, polished stone or shellacked plaster. In each case the front face should be mechanically true, without ripples or dents. The surface is set upon a table so that the trued edge overhangs by ¼ in. and it is useful if some plastic guttering is set beneath the outer edge of the table to collect any plaster which might otherwise fall on to the floor area where one must walk or stand.

First the profile must be cut accurately to one's design and a similar wooden profile cut slightly larger so that it increases the rigidity of the template when backed up to it without interfering with the form of the plaster. The two templates are then bolted on to the plough. The plaster is mixed in the usual way and poured on to the surface and the plough and template moved through it, ensuring that the plough is run against the leading edge of the sledging surface. A straight run will thus be guaranteed. As the plaster is setting the profile will plough it to shape; any extra plaster necessary to fill any hollow areas may be taken from that which builds up on the template, but for very fine finishes it may be necessary to add a fresh mix of plaster.

This process can be varied by modifying the edge against which the plough runs. To produce arcs of a circle the plough is attached to a radial arm, and when the arm is fixed to a pivot with the plough at the opposite end moved through setting plaster the result will be a curved sledged shape. If the plough runs not on a flat surface, but on one which undulates, the curved shape will also undulate.

If very small shapes are to be ploughed the forward pressure of the plough may overcome the bond between the casting surface and the

35 Sledging—view from in front of the template

36 Sledging—view from behind the template

setting plaster in which case small holes should be drilled in the sledging bench and headless nails glued into them, cut to a length of about half an inch so that they will not interfere with the profiled surface of the plaster. The nails will stop the plaster from sliding during the sledging process. When the plaster has finished setting and has cooled, it can be lifted from the bench and the nails removed. The holes which remain can be filled with plaster until they are required once more.

Ploughs or sledges can be made of wood or of metal, preferably nonferrous, so that they do not rust. The metal types are more accurate, but for some work one may have to design and make one's own plough. Time and expense would not usually permit making a metal plough suitable for one job only and a wooden plough will be accurate for a short time. They tend to deteriorate with use as the wood may split or distort with wetting and drying which cannot be avoided in use.

Making templates

Metal templates should be made of a metal which can be cut with relative ease, e.g. zinc litho plates. If it is no more than ⅛ in. thick most hand tools will cut out the basic shape quite quickly, but large profiles will not be rigid enough to produce an accurate model. Metal templates are therefore usually backed with wooden templates, cut so that the edge of the wooden profile is about ¼ in. larger than the metal on every profile edge. When the two are fastened together, the wooden edge must not interfere with the action of the metal one. The edge of the metal template should be bevelled so that the leading edge is sharp and accurate. This can

37 Base plate for an oval model

38 Modelling the core against which the model can be cast to produce the interior surface of an oval wash-basin using a template profile and the base plate to define the form

39 Modelling the exterior surface of the model of the wash-basin

be done by drawing the desired shape on to the metal and cutting to about ⅛ in. of this line with a jig saw or fret saw. File off the burr left by the saw and then file back to the line at an angle of 45° so that the drawn line is the cutting edge of the profile. When using thinner materials, this bevelling may not be possible or necessary and accurate cutting with a fret saw and truing with a file may be all that is needed.

Rubber moulds

If the plaster model has been difficult to achieve or is so complex that it has taken a long time to model, it will be worth taking one or two precautions to safeguard all that effort. Rather than make a mould direct from the model with all the attendant risks of damaging the model or even worse of miscalculating and locking the model and mould together, a rubber cast from the plaster can be taken. Two types of rubber are available for this purpose, a cold casting usually white rubber, which air sets and can therefore be used once only, or a hot rubber such as vynamould which is red. The latter rubber can be reused by cutting it up and melting it in a heater designed for the purpose. This type of heater is thermostatically controlled to avoid overheating the rubber. Nevertheless, the rubber must be heated to 150°C before it will melt and great care must be taken to avoid being splashed as at this temperature the rubber will cause a severe burn if it comes into contact with the skin.

Whichever rubber is used, one should be aware that it can cause skin irritation and dermatitis in some cases, so it is a good idea to use rubber or polythene gloves when handling the material.

When casting rubbers against plaster, it is not necessary to use a release agent. The plaster should be thoroughly dry and if a drier is available in which the plaster can lie for twenty-four hours or more, it should be used or the model set in a warm dry place until when cool, it feels neutral rather than cold.

To strengthen the model further, one might decide to resin impregnate it. See page 68.

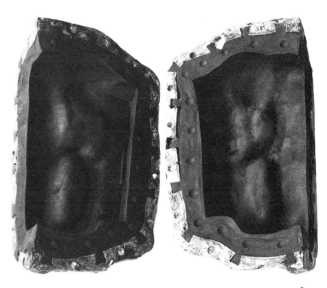

40 Vynamold and plaster mould. The object has first been covered in a 1 in. thickness of clay with the dovetails modelled on to it. Plaster is poured to produce a two-piece mould. One side of the clay is removed and the rubber poured into the two-piece mould with the model held in place by the other clay-side. Then the second half of the clay is removed and the second section of rubber poured in

Making a plaster backing

The model may now have a cast taken from it using hot or cold rubber. Normally the rubber is built up to a depth of between ¼ in. and ½ in. When the rubber is set plaster is poured over the back so that it will form a solid support for the flexible rubber when the model has been removed. Casting the rubber is very simple because it will release from any undercuts. It may be poured over the dry model, but retaining walls may be advisable to prevent the rubber from flowing too far beyond the edge of the model. The back of the rubber should be slightly textured to form a register and key for the plaster support. If possible, the plaster should run down to the surface upon which the model is set so the walls may have to be moved to allow the plaster support to run beyond the rubber. Depending on the form of the model it may be necessary to divide the plaster support although the rubber mould will peel off the model without being divided. If it should prove difficult to peel off one can cut the rubber with a sharp scalpel, being careful not to damage the model.

The purpose of making a rubber mould is to produce a second model which is perfect in every detail. The rubber should have no air bubbles trapped against the plaster model, but if any are found they should be filled with clay before casting the second plaster model. The rubber mould is then set in its plaster supports which are tied together if necessary. Plaster is mixed in the usual way and then poured into the rubber mould. When it has set and cooled the mould is opened and the plaster model is revealed. It can be used to produce a plaster production mould after it has been sealed either by resin impregnation or by soaping it until it is waterproof.

Resin impregnation

Two alternatives to soaping the plaster model are shellacking or resin impregnation. They serve the same purpose, but increase the hardness of the model. Shellac is a varnish mixed with spirit. It should be brought to the consistency of water by thinning with methylated spirits, and allowed to dry for at least half an hour between coats. Two coats should be sufficient for most purposes. The result should be a shiny, hard plaster surface with no alteration to the plaster model detail. The shellacked surface may be very lightly soaped as a further precaution before casting.

Resin impregnation produces a durable model, but is hazardous. The resin is supplied with a separate hardener which is extremely dangerous as it is carcinogenic. When using either of these ingredients, it must be done in a well ventilated room, preferably in an extraction booth, wearing goggles, a respirator with a fume filter and using disposable rubber or polythene gloves. Two coats of resin should be sufficient when applied to an absolutely dry model and the model should also be allowed to dry between coats applied with a soft paint brush and finally cured in a warm place not exceeding 70°C to avoid cracking the model. This is normally done in a thermostatically controlled oven.

Soaping the model

If soap is to be used it should be soft soap (otherwise called potter's size) produced for this purpose. The soap should be heated, sieved if necessary and dissolved in hot water until it is the consistency of thin cream. The resulting solution is applied to the dry plaster, using a natural sponge which is kept for the purpose. Do not wash the sponge but leave it in the soft soap solution. The soap is applied and when dried the model is washed with clean water and a sponge. When dry again the model is soaped once more. It should be soaped and sponged off at least three times to ensure that it is completely sealed. The resultant surface should be smooth and free from any lumps or streaks of soap which may be absorbed by the fresh plaster used to make the mould and weaken it. Crevices in the model may retain soap bubbles and these must be removed with a small paint brush or wooden modelling tool. In so doing ensure that the surface beneath remains properly soaped.

When soaping is completed a decision must be taken about the way the mould should be divided to ensure the release of the model. Sometimes the model may be designed to produce a one or two-piece mould and severe undercuts avoided to simplify the mould.

Casting

Having decided where the mould is to be divided and which piece is to be cast first the walls or cottles are set in place. For large curved walls a flexible clean plastic sheet is most suitable as the plaster does not stick to it. For complex shapes plaster strips or sheets, a byproduct of the casting process, are ideal. Each time plaster is mixed there is some surplus plaster left in the jug which should be poured on to a sheet of glass from which it will release when set. The resulting pancakes should be kept and when required they can be cut to shape and shellacked or soaped to form walls around the model. Small gaps between the model and such walls should be sealed on the outside with clay. When the walls are all in place and secure the plaster is weighed out, blended and poured.

When pouring the plaster avoid doing so directly on to the model if possible. Instead pour it into the gap between the model and the wall or cottle, so that the plaster will rise around the model and gradually flood it, excluding the air as it does so. Air bubbles trapped against the model can thus be avoided or at least minimized.

After casting the first part of the mould the walls may be removed and any plaster which has crept underneath can be removed by cutting it away from the parent plaster. It should release from the surface of the model quite easily. The edges which will form the walls of the next area to be cast must be trimmed and natches cut to provide a register for the next piece of mould, then soaped. It is advisable to check that each piece of the mould will release from the model before casting the subsequent part. This is usual in the case of complex moulds of say six or more pieces. The mould making should proceed until the whole model is cast. Some pieces are designed to be cast by pouring slip into the mould through a hole in the back or base of the model. To produce this hole a soaped conical bung should be set against that surface of the model where the pouring hole will be located when the time comes for that surface to be cast. The smaller face of the bung should be set against the model so that the bung can be removed from the outside of the model.

When casting has been completed the last piece of mould to be cast is taken from the model followed by each subsequent piece, the first part to

41 The handle set up for casting the second half of the handle mould

42 The model of the handle and two pieces of the finished mould

43 The cup model, various model handles and the cup moulds

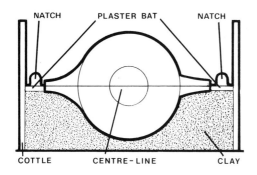

NATCH PLASTER BAT NATCH

COTTLE CENTRE-LINE CLAY

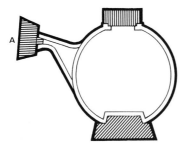

A

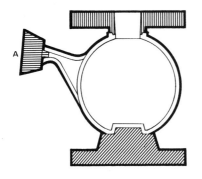

A

44 Making the mould for a teapot
Top: view from the end showing natches in position
Middle: view from side with
spares in position
Bottom: view from side with
base cast and top cast around
smaller spare in the top

be cast being the last to be removed until the model is free from the
mould. The mould should be cleaned of any unnecessary projections of
plaster to leave a smooth outer surface free of bits which might break off
and be included in the clay cast. If any accident has occurred, this
procedure may have to be repeated with another model cast from the
rubber mould.

At this stage, the mould contains a lot of water and may warp during
drying unless the pieces of the mould are assembled and tied tightly
together until thoroughly dry. If the mould is to be used for slip casting it
must be left to dry for two or three days at about 40°C and even if it is to
be used for pressing plastic clay it will need to dry for at least
twenty-four hours. In either case, the first one or two casts from a new
mould may be imperfect as they tend to pick up fragments of plaster
from seams, etc. and may pick up traces of soap. Allow moulds to cool
slowly to avoid cracking due to thermal shock.

8 Throwing and jolleying

Throwing from a hump

If a number of similar pieces are to be thrown, i.e. small bowls or jars, the clay is wedged in the normal way in a piece large enough for eight or twelve pieces, then set upon the wheel and centered. The cone is formed on a cylindrical shape from about two-thirds of the height measured from the base. The first pot is formed from the top part of the cone and when complete a groove is cut with a turning tool beneath the pot allowing enough clay for the base of the form. The pot is cut from the hump, either by using a wide spatula which cuts through the clay and leaves the pot on the blade of the spatula, or with a cutting cord with a toggle at one end only. This is offered up against the groove as the cone revolves and the loose end allowed to twist round the clay: as the line tightens, the toggle is pulled and the wire drawn through the clay as the wheel is halted, cutting the pot from the cone to leave an oyster shell ripple in the clay. The intention is to produce a pot where the base need not be turned, the cut giving a decorative finish to it.

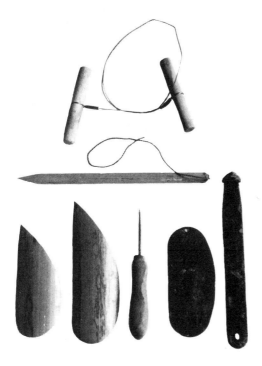

45 Throwing tools

46

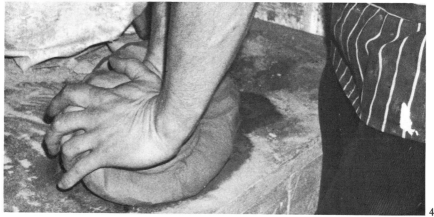

47

48

49

46 Spiral wedging 1

47 Spiral wedging 2

48 The hump centred ready to throw the first pot

49 Throwing a bowl on the hump

50 Sponging the interior

51 The bowl cut off the hump

One other method using a cutting wire with two toggles is to place the wire on the far side of the pot, pulling the toggles to the front so that the wire runs round the clay and then crossing them over. Hands on the toggles should then be changed and pulled in opposite directions. The wire will cut through the clay to leave a ripple pattern with the centre of the rings at the side of the pot. In this process the loop of wire becomes smaller as it is drawn towards one by the outward pull on the toggles.

When the pot has been cut away the top of the cone is rounded off and another pot thrown. The process from the start of one pot to the start of another takes less time than is necessary to describe it. As the pots should be completely formed when they are cut off this type of throwing is an economical studio production method.

52 A lid being cut off the hump

53 The characteristic oyster shell pattern produced using a twisted cutting wire with only one toggle

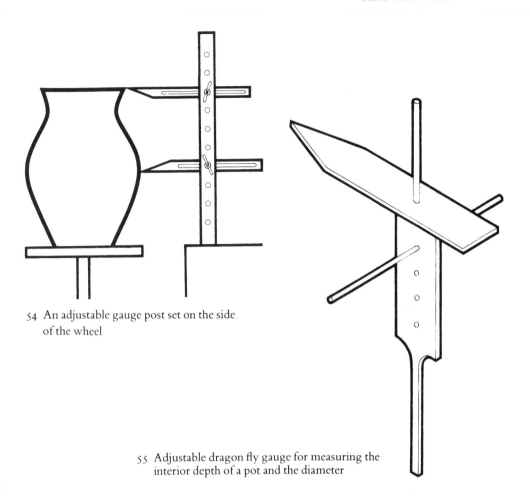

54 An adjustable gauge post set on the side
of the wheel

55 Adjustable dragon fly gauge for measuring the
interior depth of a pot and the diameter

When throwing standard sizes, measuring posts should be set up; for instance, in front to check the height of each piece and another to check the maximum diameter. In time one may become able to assess the height of each pot as it is thrown, but this facility takes time to acquire. When taking measurements of the inside and outside of forms a pair of callipers is needed. Bow callipers are useful for measuring, as in use only the tip to each calliper arm comes near the clay. When being used to measure the inside top diameter, the arm should be crossed over so that the tips of the arms point outwards.

The inside height of a pot can be measured by a gauge, which is set when the first pot is thrown and the position of the horizontal bar fixed on the vertical pointer. In Japan a measuring tool called a dragon fly is used to measure simultaneously the depth and diameter of a pot, but the potter must ensure that the vertical arm is over the centre of the pot.

Templates or ribs are used to assist in the forming of thrown shapes. They vary in size and shape, some are more or less standard and are used for initial forming of the clay, whilst others are made to assist in the forming of special shapes, particularly narrow necked forms. Not all potters use these as they prefer the spiralling form created by the fingers.

56 Throwing a bottle using a rib on the outside

In production throwing ribs can speed up the forming process, avoid irregularities in the surface, remove any scum which can build up on the surface of the clay and when used on the interior of the pot they check the shape, diameter and depth of the form. (When using a rib on the outside of the form it is usually held in the right hand.)

The templates are made of wood as this is sympathetic to the clay, comfortable to handle and is quite easily shaped. The edge to be used against the clay is bevelled to create a thin and definite edge. When in use any scum scraped off the clay should be wiped off the template at intervals.

Long handled ribs used to shape the inside of narrow necked pots must be made of fine grained wood to avoid the likelihood of it splitting when in use. This type of template is held inside the form in one hand whilst the other supports and works the clay on the outside—immediately opposite the point where the pressure is being exerted. Care must be taken as the interior rib is manipulated so that the narrow top is not damaged by the long handle.

57 Making the narrow neck

58 Shaping the interior using a template

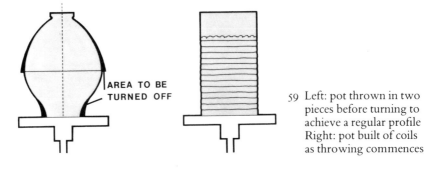

59 Left: pot thrown in two
pieces before turning to
achieve a regular profile
Right: pot built of coils
as throwing commences

Throwing

A pot can be thrown in stages and the separate sections joined together when leather hard, or the top can be thrown, set to one side and then the lower section thrown. Both should be thicker than the finished section is intended to be. The bottom section is left on the wheel and whilst still soft the top is luted to it and the complete pot rethrown. In this way centering a massive amount of clay can be avoided. Alternatively, one can throw the bottom section of the pot and lute round the top a thick rope of clay, 4 or 5 ins high. The coil is then thrown as if it were the top of the pot. This process can be continued, coil upon coil, until the pot is the desired size and form. Apart from the question of having the ability to throw large pots, the irregularities inherent in these throwing techniques can be regarded as qualities of the finished pots.

Jolleying

Jolleying can be regarded as an extension of throwing with the aid of profiles, the outer profile being a strong plaster hollow mould and the inner one attached to a swinging arm which presses up against the clay in the mould when gradually lowered.

An adjustable stop is located near the fulcrum of the jolley arm so that the stop position of the profile can be preset and the thickness of the clay wall of the form will be regulated without the need to measure each piece. The whole machine must be set up carefully so that the profile is correctly aligned with the mould to produce the desired form and section. The profile can be of metal or even wood, but plastics such as perspex are more easily shaped. Whatever material is used it should be

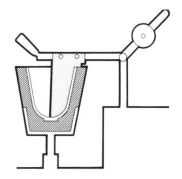

60 Jolleying: section through the template
and mould

61 Metal cup heads used to hold moulds during
jolleying

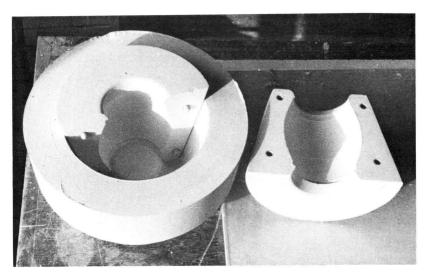

62 A two-piece jolley mould showing the case which holds the two parts
together during jolleying

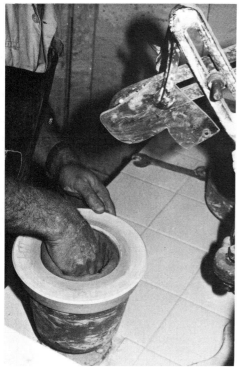

63 Jolleying in a one-piece mould—the clay being hollowed

64 The clay being thrown in the mould

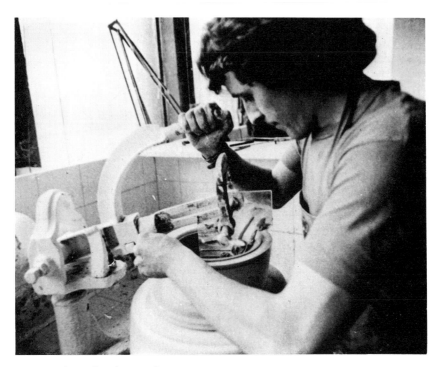

65 Forming using the template

66 The template raised

67 The shaping completed

about ⅜ in. thick and bevelled so that the bevelled edge leads the clay in towards the shaping edge. The profile must be rigid so that it is not distorted by the pressure of the clay.

The mould in jolleying is held in a tapered metal cup head attached to a vertical spindle so that it revolves like a potter's wheel. A measured amount of clay is thrown as a hollow blank that is then set in the mould which in turn is placed in the metal cup head. The inner profile is offered up to the clay whilst the mould is spinning and the pressure of the inner template gradually increased until the final thickness of the clay form has been defined. During this part of the process the profile presses upon the clay and any excess travels on to the template or to the top of the mould and must from time to time be removed with a sponge. The shaping of the clay is assisted as in throwing with the use of water as a lubricant.

The process can be carried out with automated equipment in which case the inner profile is replaced with a roller head which rotates mechanically to produce a squeezing action against the clay. Such roller heads are made of metal and may be heated which has the effect of plasticizing the clay as it is shaped as well as speeding up drying of the finished piece.

In all cases, it is usual to have several moulds so that several pieces can be made consecutively and if a rotary drier is used the process can be organized so that by the time the last mould has been used the first clay shape has dried sufficiently for it to be removed from the mould which can be used again. In smaller workshops the moulds and profiles may vary so that batches of different forms can be made. As the quantity of clay to be used should be measured, it makes sense to work the various moulds and profiles in batches of similar if not identical sizes.

Turning

When turning standard shapes a clay chuck, usually thrown (see ill. 68), should be made to support the pot from within during turning. The chuck should be allowed to dry until it is leather hard and the pot set upon it and levelled. Narrow necked pots should be set in a hollow chuck which supports the body of the form without the top of the pot touching the wheel head. Excess clay is turned off with a wooden or metal turning tool, available in a variety of shapes from manufacturers but most potters make their own. They are often made from strips of mild steel cut into pieces about 6 ins long with the ends turned at right angles to form a z shape. The ends are then ground down, preferably with an electric grinder to form either a triangular or leaf shape, and the tool is given a cutting edge by bevelling the outer edge and finishing with a file to remove any burrs resulting from the grinding. Bamboo turning tools are more like knife blades cut and bevelled to a straight or curved cutting edge. Both steel and bamboo tools keep their edge quite well but commercial tungsten tipped turning tools may justify their relative expense if it is necessary to do a lot of very precise turning.

When turning porcelain ensure than the clay chuck does not stain the pot. It is expensive to use porcelain for the chuck, but this may be unavoidable if the only other clay causes staining. Soft absorbent paper can be dampened and used to cover that part of the chuck which comes into contact with the pot. The paper must be soft enough to allow the pot to grip the chuck. In addition, turning can be used to decorate the clay pot. If a springy cutting tool is used (they are made of thin flexible metal strips), it will bounce upon the clay to create a series of chattering marks. The rhythm created during this process is unique and cannot be

68 Left: section through a thrown clay chuck suitable for supporting a bowl during turning
Right: section through a thrown clay chuck suitable for supporting a narrow necked bottle

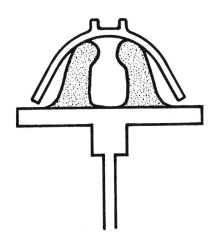
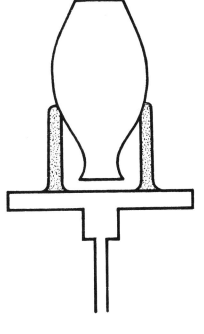

69 Lathe turning clay, the bead on the foot of the pot (photographed from above)

70 Lathe turning clay, using a straight edge profile (photographed from above)

simulated. At first the results may be uneven, but with a little practice it will be possible to regulate the chattering to create an even rhythm.

The foot of the pot turned whilst the clay is still soft is essentially different from a foot turned from leather hard clay.

Jiggering

This term is used to describe the process of making flatware by means of a mould and profile.

The clay is first 'batted out', i.e. made into a flat disc by means of a batting out machine, which is a motor-driven horizontal wheel with a head or top of plaster about 3 or 4 ins thick. A predetermined weight of clay is knocked roughly into a thick round pancake shape and set upon the batting head. The wheel is rotated and a flat profile swung down on to it to spread out the clay into a disc of uniform thickness determined by an adjustable stop on the profile arm.

The disc is picked up and set upon a mould of the plate, which is designed to produce the interior profile of the plate and can be described as a 'hump mould'. The mould is set into a metal cup head and spun whilst a profile designed to form the back of the plate is swung down on to the clay and will simultaneously form any footring which is a feature of the design of the plate.

Profiles are best made of thick plastic such as perspex about ½ in. thick. The edge which is to form the clay is cut to shape with a band saw or fret saw. The working edge is bevelled so that when the template is offered up to the clay the rotation of the jigger leads the clay into the bevel and the clay is finally formed by the outer edge of the profile. The template must be large enough to be held firmly in the jigger and thick enough not to flex when it is forming the clay.

Automated plate-making machines like automated jolleys use metal roller heads instead of profiles.

It may be necessary to dry certain plates upside down if they would otherwise shrink and lock on to the plate mould.

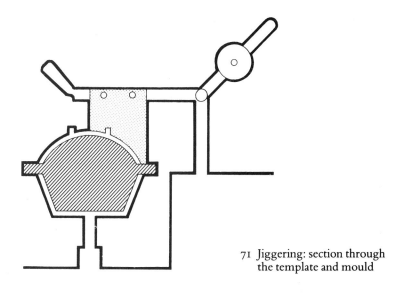

71 Jiggering: section through the template and mould

9   Press moulding and casting

The purpose of a mould is either to support the clay during the forming process because it will not support itself until it is dryer than this forming process allows, or to achieve repetitive forms and textures which do not lend themselves to construction by hand. The mould material is usually plaster of Paris although bisquit clay, wood and sand are still used for certain products and the two latter materials were essential before the invention of plaster of Paris in 1750. Some of the methods of fabricating clay shapes using moulds will be described here.

Press moulding

Clays for pressing should be plastic enough to bend into the shape of the mould without cracking. This can be achieved by using softer clay than free standing forms demand, although the increase in water content may require the inclusion of grog in the clay to aid drying and avoid distortion when the clay is taken from the mould. These clays can be less plastic than throwing clays, and bone china, which is notoriously difficult to throw, can be press moulded. Indeed, many industrially produced pieces, i.e. large platters, were hand-pressed in bone china although much less frequently today. The forms to be pressed may be made in separate pieces and luted together before firing. The moulds should have at least one surface open so that one can get one's hand into all parts of it to ensure that the clay is pressed well up against the plaster. Pieces pressed separately can be luted together whilst both are in their respective moulds, or one can be removed and set upon another that remains in its mould which supports the lower form until that is strong enough to support the upper section. It is vital to ensure that the mould is so formed that it will permit the clay to shrink during drying without hanging on any projection, as that part of the moulded clay which is hooked on to part of the mould may prove too weak to withstand the forces exerted upon it by the weight of clay it is carrying and it will crack. The mould should be inverted as soon as the clay shows evidence of coming away from it to avoid cracking. Obviously the form should not include large projections into the interior volume around which the clay is pressed because as it shrinks three-dimensionally it will become locked on to the plaster and must be cut apart to release it.

Pressing can be carried out in two ways. The first is to roll out the clay into a sheet and lay the sheet of clay into the mould. Water and a clean sponge will be needed to ease the clay into the deepest part of the mould and into any deep recesses in the sides. The clay must be plastic and soft enough to stretch into these parts of the mould without any cracking of the surface which finally comes up against the mould. Small cracks are sometimes tolerated because they can be modelled out when the piece comes from the mould.

The second method also requires soft clay, not necessarily as plastic as with the pressing method. The clay is laid into the mould in pieces about the size of a fist. It is then smeared across the mould and the next handful is set over some of the clay already in the mould and spread outwards so that the layers overlap. The process is continued until the pressing is complete. The interior must then be modelled using tools and templates to smooth and compact it.

In the first method, the thickness of the clay is regulated largely by the thickness of the clay pancake rolled out. In the second method, the thickness of the clay must be modelled as it is smoothed in the mould. To check the thickness a needle pushed through the clay should be used until the plaster resisting the pressure can be felt. A small cork or rubber disc can be put on the needle so that it can be used as a gauge to achieve the correct thickness.

Casting

Clays which are to be used as casting bodies may be less plastic than throwing clays, but whatever composition is used should be tested for finished colour and glaze reaction. To make the body into a casting slip, it must be slaked or mixed with water to the consistency of cream. Without further addition the resulting slip will have a water content in the region of 40 per cent plus. It will be realized that the mould becomes wet very quickly and must be dried between each casting.

When fired to maturing temperature, the finished piece will have shrunk by 20 per cent or more and is likely to warp during drying and firing. Whilst water casting can be useful for some castings where the excessive shrinkage is not a disadvantage, it is preferable to use a process called deflocculation which reduces the amount of water required to change the body to a liquid. The two most common deflocculants are sodium silicate and soda ash, which must be added in carefully controlled proportions into the water in which the clay will be broken down. Normally deflocculants are required in amounts less than 0.5 per cent of the weight of the clay.

To determine the exact amount of deflocculant required for a body one must conduct an experiment to determine the deflocculation curve, a graph which indicates the optimum amount of deflocculation and water necessary to make the clay liquid (Appendix 5). The process of deflocculation is not fully understood, but the most acceptable theory is that the deflocculant changes some of the electrical charges in the atoms of clay material so that instead of attracting they repel each other.

Sodium silicate decreases thixotropy by making the clay particles repel each other and the soda ash increases the power of the repulsion. The pint weight for most slips is between 34/35 oz to the pint (imperial), 28 oz to the pint (USA), 170 g for 100 cc.

The chemical condition of the casting slip may be affected by the alkalinity or acidity (measured as the ph) of the water. If one is regularly using casting slips, it will help to keep the batches stable and similar in character if only one source of water is used. As clays change their character with age, so casting slips will change if stored for prolonged

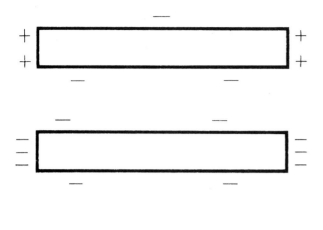

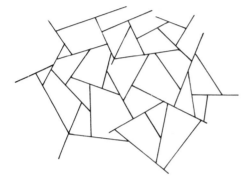

72 Top to bottom:
Section through a platelet of
clay showing electrical charges
a) normal
b) deflocculated
Section through a clay layer
a) normal
b) deflocculated

periods. A batch of casting slip should be checked each day to measure its pint weight (to see if there has been any loss of water through evaporation) and thixotropy. A pint measure (100 cc) and a torsion viscometer, the use of which is described in Appendix 4, is needed. If the slip has increased in pint weight water can be added to the batch in small amounts at a time to bring it to the correct pint weight. If it has become lighter, more of the body should be added. The amounts to be added must be calculated against the amount of slip remaining in the tank or bucket, preferably calibrated to indicate the number of pints of slip remaining. This assessment will show the amount of clay or water needed to restore the pint weight. If on restoring the pint weight the thixotropy is too great, more deflocculant must be added, although one must be aware that any minor error in assessing the remaining volume of slip may result in too much deflocculant being added. As can be imagined, one can add clay, water and deflocculant all day and still not get the slip exactly right. Indeed, too much deflocculant will result in the slip starting to flocculate, i.e. the thixotropy will increase (Appendix 5).

It is advisable to avoid the need to adjust existing casting slips by making up only what can be used in three or four days and storing it in an airtight container. It is not a good idea to add spare casting slip back into the batch. In industry, a small amount of dry deflocculated body is sometimes added to a fresh batch but in the quantities likely to be made (five to eight gallons maximum), it is inadvisable because the resulting mixture may become unstable. When a batch of slip goes seriously awry, i.e. pint weight is correct but thixotropy cannot be adjusted, one can only discard the batch and start again.

Bone china casting slips become unstable with storage and must be used within a week or so, or the chance taken of having to discard part of the batch. Bone china is expensive, so throwing away quantities of deflocculated unstable slip is to be avoided.

Casting slips which work ideally will cast to the required thickness within about twenty minutes, drain from the mould without leaving smears or 'wreaths' of slip on the inside of the cast, release from the mould without sticking and have sufficient green strength to retain their shape during drying.

Casting time is determined by the porosity of the plaster of Paris mould which should be dry, but cool; the water content in the slip and the particle size of the body should be such that the water can travel through the casting clay so that a satisfactory thickness can build up during the casting time.

Wreathing is usually a sign of a too low thixotropy of the slip which may be due to a shortage of water or deflocculant, or too much deflocculant.

Sticking to the mould may be due to some characteristic of the mould surface (soft soap residue from the mould) or the incorrect amount of deflocculant or the mould may be damp.

Green strength depends upon the formulation of the body: plastic clays provide it.

Each mould should be dried after each casting and a thermostatically controlled drier is a great help. The temperature within the drier should maintain the temperature at about 70°C with a flow of air to remove the water-laden atmosphere, a fan heater fitted to the drier and controlled by a thermostat can provide these conditions. The mould should be allowed to cool before casting.

The slip should be taken from the tank in a quantity sufficient for the mould or moulds in which it is intended to cast. Sieve the slip through an 80 mesh sieve to remove any lumps and then charge the mould. Check it during the casting time and top up as necessary. When cast to the correct thickness drain the mould and return the residual slip to the tank. Leave the mould upside down to drain thoroughly.

When the cast is firm enough to remove from the mould, dismantle the mould and cut away any spares with a sharp knife or scalpel and sponge away any mould seams. Reassemble the empty mould and fasten it tightly together and replace in the drier. Lute together any separately cast pieces by cross-hatching surfaces to be joined and coating with slip or water. Clean the joins with a sponge and set the finished cast to dry. If the piece includes a lid, set this in the top as soon as possible, as it will help to keep the piece in shape. Dry the ware slowly and evenly, and avoid draughts which can produce uneven drying and warpage. When thoroughly dry the piece can be decorated and then fired or fired without decoration.

All plaster moulds deteriorate with use and deflocculated slips corrode the plaster more rapidly than clay-water slips. Corrosion removes detailed modelling, softens the overall appearance of the form and also eats away the surface of the mould. Small air bubbles are then usually revealed just beneath this surface, which will show in the cast as a surface covered with small pimples. Unless this quality is liked the mould is now useless and must be discarded. New moulds can be made from the original model.

Press moulding and slip casting can be carried out in coloured clays, textured clays and a variety of materials that will produce decorative qualities in the finished piece without the necessity of applying the decoration in a separate process.

The casting surface of the mould can be decorated with trailed slip, painted colour, incised lines, etc., and these qualities will be picked up in the cast. They will also be picked up in subsequent casts so do not embark on modifying the mould unless it is intended to maintain the quality through several casts until the mould has become useless.

10   Theory and practice of glaze composition

It would be possible to manufacture glazes from pure elements, but the refinement necessary to convert natural minerals to their separate elements would make the resultant materials very expensive and the process unnecessarily complex. It is cheaper and more convenient to select certain naturally occurring materials which include the elements wanted and combine them in carefully designed proportions to produce the desired composition after firing.

Most naturally occurring materials include a mixture of elements and it may be necessary to separate some of these. Very small quantities of foreign materials in an otherwise pure deposit of a single mineral are called trace elements and may be present in such small quantities as to be too insignificant to concern most users. These trace elements may be very important for the ceramist as they can be responsible for producing highly desirable effects on a glaze.

Glazes can be written down in various ways:

1. As a recipe of materials (usually in percentages or weights).
2. As a percentage composition of the compounds present in the fired glaze.
3. As a molecular composition of the fired glaze known as an empirical formula.

System 1 tells one what to put into the glaze providing there is access to materials identical to those listed and will always be used when making up a glaze batch. The recipe is simple to follow. Systems 2 and 3 tell one what the fired glaze will be made of. System 2 is rarely used although chemical analysis of materials is often expressed in this way and it may be required if the thermal expansion of the glaze is to be calculated. System 3 is commonly used where an expression of the finished glaze is required. If a glaze were to be analyzed after firing, the results would be written in three columns, as a molecular formula.

$$RO \qquad R_2O_3 \qquad RO_2$$
$$\text{basic} \qquad \text{amphoteric} \qquad \text{acid}$$

This system of writing down the oxides which appear in the finished glaze is variously known as a Seger Formula (after Herman Seger 1839-94 who developed the system), an empirical formula or a molecular formula. It will be referred to in using the term molecular formula because it is a constant reminder that we are considering the amounts of the various materials as molecular equivalents. In many cases, a figure written down will be less than a complete molecule and, as stated on page 30, there can be no quantity of a compound less than one molecule in size. This type of formula is a theoretical composition and it is simpler to allow parts of a molecule in the mathematical system.

In the first column those elements which have combined with 1 atom of oxygen can be found; in the second column those which have combined with 1½ atoms of oxygen (this is easier to understand and more accurately described as 2 atoms of the element combining with 3 atoms of oxygen) and the third column lists those elements which have been combined with 2 atoms of oxygen. The columns represent also the various activities of the ingredients: in the first column the fluxes and colouring elements will be found, in the second column the alumina which stabilizes the melting process and helps to keep the glaze from running off the pot during firing, and in the third column the silica, which is a glass forming material, is set.

Characteristics of the three groups of oxides used in molecular formulae

Metallic oxides	Neutral oxides	Non-metallic oxides
Basic oxides	Amphoteric oxides	Acid oxides
RO column (monovalent elements)	R_2O_3 column (trivalent elements)	RO_2 column (tetravalent elements)
R_2O column (divalent elements)		

Network modifiers		Network co-formers	Network formers
BaO	MnO	Al_2O_3	SiO_2
CaO	Na_2O		
CdO	PbO		
FeO	SrO		$\star B_2O_3$
K_2O	ZnO		
Li_2O	ZrO_2		
MgO			

$\star B_2O_3$ is sometimes written in the R_2O_3 column, but as it is a network, i.e. glass forming material, it can also be written in the RO_2 column.

For ease of comparison the RO column is always written to total one molecular equivalent and when representing a clay body the R_2O_3 column is brought to a total of one. Either of these systems is described as a unity formula. By the comparison of proportions of amphoteric and acid oxides compared to the basic oxides, it will be possible with a little experience to ascertain the likely performance of a glaze when it is written as a unity molecular formula. The system tells little about the finished state or appearance of the glaze and what should be mixed together to make the glaze; neither does it tell one the exact firing temperature or atmosphere.

It does, however, provide an analysis of the final glaze and to this, if they have been analyzed, materials which are available can be matched.

Conversely, if one has a glaze made up of certain ingredients and one or more of those is no longer available, a molecular formula, can be produced from an analysis of the ingredients. The missing oxides can then be provided by a substitute material. A direct substitution is not always possible because the only available material with the necessary ingredients may include unwanted oxides or those already supplied within the recipe. In this circumstance, a new recipe must be created to produce the desired molecular formula.

A further use of the molecular formula is that it allows one to create a theoretical glaze from available and analyzed material by reference to limit formulae and phase diagrams.

Limit formulae are published results of experiments to determine the maximum and minimum ratios of flux to amphoteric to acid elements which will melt at a predetermined temperature.

It will be appreciated that this system of analysis and theoretical composition requires some mathematical accuracy: but although the sums are long, they are not difficult. A calculator or a slide rule is very useful. The advantage of a calculator is that some are capable of retaining constant factors and much less notation of results is required than when using a slide rule. But if a mistake is made in a calculation using an electronic calculator it may be necessary to start again from the beginning, so it is a good idea to make a habit of writing down the complete process, at least to start with, and a method of doing this is described in Appendix 8 (bottom).

The theoretical approach is very useful and is sometimes essential when tackling a problem in glaze or body formulation. It is not the only method of designing glazes nor is it sufficient in itself. Once the design has been stated as a theory it must be tried in practice. The theoretical composition will probably have to be modified in the light of practical experiments to achieve an acceptable and practical recipe.

When converting a molecular formula to a recipe a table similar to that illustrated in Apendix 8 (top) should be prepared.

The molecular formula is written at the top of the table and the oxides listed with the RO oxides on the left, then the R_2O_3 oxides and on the right the RO_2 oxides. If the RO oxides listed are alkaline a suitable feldspar can be listed in the materials column, which will give a proportion of alkaline oxides together with some alumina and silica. The molecular equivalents produced using feldspar are listed in the appropriate columns. One should aim to provide all the necessary RO oxides which should result in a shortfall in the alumina and silica. Both materials can be provided by using ball clay or china clay (kaolin): the choice between them will depend upon the physical characteristics required in the unfired glaze, but usually china clay is used. The molecular equivalents produced normally result in a shortfall of silica, which can be provided by quartz or flint.

At the end of each material line the molecular weights of each material should be listed. The weight of material to be used is the product of multiplying the required molecular equivalent of each material by the molecular weight. The recipe can be written as a percentage recipe by totalling the batch weights of materials, dividing each batch weight by the total and multiplying the product by 100:

$$\frac{\text{batch weight of one material}}{\text{total batch weight}} \times 100 = \%\text{ of the batch}$$

To convert a recipe to a molecular formula one should reverse the procedure which is described above. A chart is required similar to that in Appendix 8.

The weight of each material divided by the molecular weight gives the molecular equivalent of the material. Each material must be analyzed and across the top each oxide which is listed in the analysis of each material, can be written, but none more than once. Each oxide is present in the proportion indicated in the analysis. The process is repeated with each material in the recipe and the molecular equivalent of each oxide produced is written in the appropriate column and opposite the material producing it. When all the oxides have been calculated the molecular equivalent of each oxide is totalled and the oxides listed in columns, i.e. RO_1, R_2O_3, RO_2.

The RO column is then brought to unity, i.e. totalling one molecular equivalent. This is done by totalling the molecular equivalent in the RO column and dividing the molecular equivalent of each oxide in the formula by this total. Thus the RO column is brought to a total of one and the other oxides are proportionately changed.

Unity formulae allow for the easy comparison between one glaze and another.

Eutectics

When a mixture of ceramic materials is fired the different materials included in the mixture melt at different temperatures. Some melt only at high temperatures whilst others melt with very little heat. A material which is resistant to heat is called a refractory material. As one material melts the more refractory one is surrounded by a glass of the less refractory one. Fortunately not all materials behave in this insular way. Those mixed together may melt at a temperature below the melting point of either materials when separate. This phenomenon is called eutectic behaviour and is fundamental to the properties of ceramic materials when heated. Tables of eutectics of two or more materials are published and may be graphically presented in the form of phase diagrams.

Phase diagrams

With two materials mixed in predetermined proportions a graph of the melting temperature of each sample mix can be drawn, taking the proportional mixes listed along the base, starting with 100 per cent of each material at opposite ends of the base. The vertical axis indicates the temperature. The eutectic point will be the lowest point on the graph. When the various melting points are joined together the line produced separates the liquid phase (above the line) from the solid phase (below the line). See ill. 73.

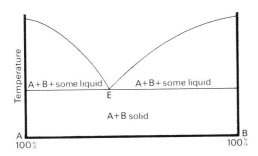

73 A binary phase diagram

Triaxial blends

Three materials can be mixed in predetermined proportions (ill. 74) and a three-dimensional graph is produced with the upright axis indicating the temperature (ill. 75). In this case the complete graph is a three-dimensional model which is of little use if it is represented as a drawing of the model so it is normally drawn like a map with the temperature lines (called isothermic lines) serving the same purpose as contour lines in map making. To improve clarity the lines joining the proportional divisions are omitted, but they are indicated along the outer edges of the diagram. Eutectics are found at the lowest temperatures indicated, i.e. in the valleys of the landscape of the diagram.

By consulting phase diagrams the combinations of compounds can be found that will melt at the lowest temperature or alternatively the proportions of the three compounds that will melt at the temperature to which the glaze is to be fired.

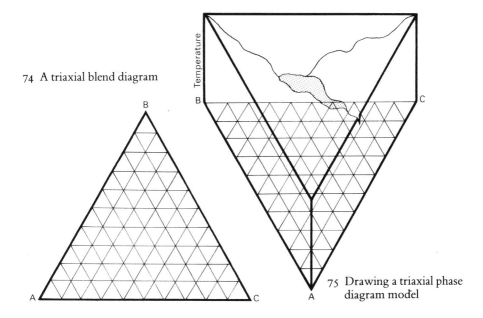

74 A triaxial blend diagram

75 Drawing a triaxial phase diagram model

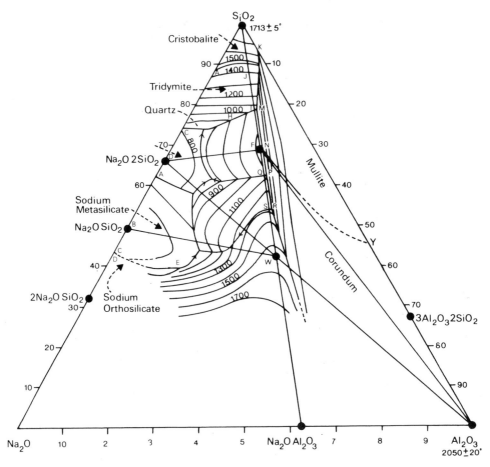

76 Phase diagram of the three elements, alumina oxide (Al₂O₃), silicon dioxide (SiO₂), sodium oxide (Na₂O), showing the liquid phase contours and the names given to the various combinations (redrawn from *Phase Diagrams for Ceramists*, p.96,)

The proportions are often written not as weights or percentages but as molecular equivalents. The phase diagram concerning three compounds indicates the various molecular equivalents and the temperatures at which that mixture will melt. The information can be extracted from the diagram and written as a molecular formula from which recipes can be composed. *Phase Diagrams for Ceramists* is an excellent source for this information.

Limit formulae

Limit formulae for various combinations of oxides can be useful because they too indicate the molecular equivalents of each oxide required to melt at a given temperature. They are generally based upon the formulae of pyrometric cones used to indicate the heat work to which a firing kiln has been subjected. As they are composed to melt at a specified temperature

Stoneware variegated glaze by Tatsuzō Shimaoko, 1976

Porcelain painted pot by Jane Osborn Smith, 1971

Porcelain bowl by Lucy Rie, *c.*1977

given a certain rate of increase in temperature they can be a useful aid in determining the correct proportions of materials required to melt to a glaze. The temperature is usually about 100°C to 150°C higher than that given for the cone for which the limit formula is designed.

The purpose and effect of firing is to fuse together the various materials in the glaze and body of the ceramic form; the temperature at which this fusion takes place varies according to the type and proportion of the materials which have been blended.

Whilst the clay body should fuse without deforming, the glazing materials should melt to a glass, without excessively running down the sides of the pot. The viscosity of the glaze is determined by the ingredients, so as alumina increases the viscosity most glazes include some of it. If a glass is to be produced in the melt some glass making material should be present and the two most commonly used are silica and boron. Something must be used to melt the glass making material at a convenient temperature and such materials are called fluxes. *A Handbook of Pottery Glazes* and *Ceramic Glazes* include limit formulae and other useful information on materials used in glazes.

Ratios of oxides in molecular equivalent glaze composition

It is necessary to consult books, catalogues and lists of ceremic materials and their uses to identify the likely range of molecular equivalents for oxides used in glazes according to the firing temperature. Such publications include guidance about the materials used to produce colour, and textures as well as those used to modify the thermal expansion of glazes and bodies. The bibliography includes some widely used books but one can also use the catalogues issued by suppliers of ceramic materials.

The following simple rules are based upon limit formulae and should be regarded only as basic guidelines. There are many examples of glazes which break one of these rules.

RO column

There should be more than one oxide except for some lead glazes, and if only sodium (Na) and potassium (K) are present the glaze will certainly craze because they have such a high thermal expansion. The greater the number of oxides the more effective will be their fluxing action. RO oxides should total one molecular equivalent.

R_2O_3 and RO_2 column

The ratio of alumina to silica should be in the region of

1 to 9 for glossy glazes
1 to 7 for semi matt glazes
1 to 5 for matt glazes

Less alumina and silica is present in low temperature glazes than in high temperature glazes.

Firing at 1300°C	0.5 mol.equiv. alumina	4.5 mol. equiv. silica
" " 1250°C	0.4 " " "	3.5 " " "
" " 1200°C	0.3 " " "	2.7 " " "
" " 1150°C	0.28 " " "	2.5 " " "

77 Fritting furnace: the ingredients are placed in a refractory crucible which is set into the circular furnace. When melted to the desired temperature the crucible is removed using the special tongs in the background. The hot liquid mix is poured into water which cools and breaks up the solidifying glassy frit

When selecting materials which will provide the oxides required, those which provide more than one, should be favoured, e.g. Cornish stone, feldspar, etc. Use single compounds to top up larger quantities of oxides in the RO column. Use china clay (kaolin) or secondary clays to provide alumina and silica.

Some secondary clays may contribute unwanted oxides. Use quartz or flint to provide the remaining silica.

RO oxides in order of fluxing effect
    Greatest   *Least*
    Li_2O, PbO, NaO, K_2O, BaO, CaO, MgO, ZnO

RO oxides in order of thermal expansion

Greatest							*Least*
Na_2O,	K_2O,	BaO,	PbO,	MgO,	CaO,	ZnO,	Li_2O
41.6	39.0	14	10.6	9.7	9.4	7.0	6.7

Oxides which are soluble must be fritted to produce an insoluble form and those which are toxic should be fritted to produce a non-toxic form. Frits may be difficult to retain in suspension in the water during application. Clay (i.e. some of the alumina/silica) component of the recipe should not be added to the frit but mixed with it in the glaze batch to aid suspension.

Feldspathic glazes

Glazes including feldspar form a large proportion of stoneware glazes. This type of material includes oxides from all three groups necessary to form a glaze and in those proportions which will melt at 1150-1300 according to the composition. The fluxing (RO R₂O) oxides may not produce a thermal expansion which is acceptable and this may have to be modified with another oxide. The ratio of silica to alumina is unlikely to be within that required for a stoneware glaze and may have to be adjusted by adding clay or quartz.

These possibilities lend themselves to a system of binary or triaxial blends to determine the correct ratio of each material for the temperature to which it is intended to fire the glaze.

Any material which includes one or more oxides can be fired in a blending system with another material providing that between them they will produce at least one oxide from the three groups, i.e. RO, R₂O₃, RO₂.

Some potters make a habit of firing line blends, triaxial blends and individual tests in their production kilns upon the clays which they intend to use to ensure that the results are the product of their normal firing schedules. Materials can be blended by weighing each substance required, or by measuring the materials by volume, e.g. teaspoon and half teaspoon measures or the slop mixing method can be used. This can be more rapid than weighing out each proportion but equally accurate if each material is mixed with the same volume of water. If the same volume of each suspension is made up in a binary mix, the following line blend can be made:

Test	No.	1	2	3	4	5	6	7	8	9	10	11
Material	A	50	50	50	50	50	50	40	30	20	10	
Material	B		10	20	30	40	50	50	50	50	50	50

Where the numbers refer to percentages by volume of the original suspensions, in order to ensure that the system is accurate the solid material must be kept in suspension by stirring or shaking the mixture before measuring each volume. Accurate measurements of volume can be made using a graduated cylinder. Number the tests as they are made. In practice No. 11 follows upon Test 6 then No. 10 and continues until Test 7.

The slop method can became very complex when used for a triaxial blend and it may be easier to weight out separately each blend.

The results of each type of test will indicate the proportions required of each material to form satisfactory glazes.

Thermal expansion

All materials expand upon heating and contract upon cooling. When the glaze is fluid it fits the clay body but as they both cool the glaze will gradually solidify and when cool and rigid it should still fit the clay. If it has shrunk more than the clay it will be stretched or 'under tension'; and is liable to produce a cracked or 'crazed' glaze surface. If the glaze has contracted much less than the body the glaze will tend to crack off the clay or 'shell' particularly on the rims or sharp edges of the pot, an effect called 'edge chipping'. As neither of these characteristics is very satisfactory the glaze should be adjusted so that it is under slight compression in case the body of the pot expands due to the absorption of atmospheric water. Stoneware bodies are less prone to this than are earthenware bodies. A glaze under slight tension will craze because the tensile stength is weak but the compressive strength is very great so the ideal to aim for is a glaze under a slight compression.

The thermal expansion of the glaze is determined by the thermal expansion of the ingredients. If the glaze is written as a percentage formula the thermal expansion of the glaze is the product of the thermal expansion of each material multiplied by the percentage of each material in the recipe. If adjusting the thermal expansion of the glaze means losing desirable qualities you will have to adjust the thermal expansion of the body. This is normally done by the crystaline silica either in the form of quartz or commercially prepared crystobalite.

The thermal expansion of the body must be determined by experiment using a thermal expansion apparatus as it is subject to variation according to the temperature and conditions under which it is fired. In the absence of this information, if the glaze crazes the thermal expansion of the glaze can be modified by progressively substituting lower thermal expansion fluxes for those with higher thermal expansion and firing each trial until one determines what glaze and body will fire and cool without crazing. Edge chipping or peeling can be rectified by increasing those materials with high thermal expansion.

As can be seen from the table on pages 135-36 the thermal expansion of the body is largely determined by the free silica in the body and the temperature to which it is fired. In some stoneware bodies which include finely ground flint or quartz the thermal expansion will be dramatically decreased if the body is overfired so that the free silica enters into the glassy phase of the body and loses all or part of its crystalline form.

Glaze making

The development of one's own range of glazes can be one of the most vital aspects of ceramic work. One can choose to work within some of the classic high temperature glazes such as celadon or chun and develop certain qualities within this range, or one may wish to examine new possibilities. It is unlikely that a totally new concept will come up but one may well discover some fresh aspect of a relatively well known technique.

The trials involved in glaze making serve the purpose not only of creating new effects but making one become aware of the qualities in glazes which the uninformed rarely appreciate. The following aspects should be considered:

1 The temperature range at which it is intended to fire the work.
2 The range of materials which work at these temperatures.
3 Previously published data referring to these temperatures and materials.

An understanding of the fired characteristics of ceramic materials can be accumulated by experiment and trial. Before the advent of scientific analysis this was the only way in which potters were able to learn about materials. By a system of binary mixing it is possible to catalogue the reactions of one material on another when mixed in varying proportions and fired at a given temperature. To run through all the possible combinations in varying proportions is time-consuming and the firing conditions must be as constant as possible. Any variation in temperature, length of firing, type of kiln, fuel or atmosphere may result in a series of trials which cannot be compared with any hope of consistent results.

Nevertheless, this system does measure the reaction of materials in a useful context and is not bound by the use of limit formulae established by other research. It may be expanded to a tertiary system where the number of possible combinations is almost overwhelming.

Most students start by taking a recipe and modifying it in some way. They take a fixed point and develop glaze or colour qualities around it and, although it is useful in building up experience and confidence, there are more demanding and stimulating ways of developing a fresh appreciation of ceramic materials.

No single technique is exclusive or sufficient in itself. Most potters need a good theoretical understanding supported by extensive practical experience.

For example, an interesting combination of two or more materials may be found that gives a new quality, but which is flawed in that the surface is not sufficiently matured. If one fires higher the clay body may be damaged. It is necessary to know what to add to the recipe to flux the mix at a convenient temperature. A list of ceramic materials which states the melting points, or published experiments detailing the eutectic of various mixes may be consulted and a suitable material selected. Or one can simply vary the ratio between one of the materials and the others in the mixture. No matter how well the theory is researched it will still be necessary to make some experimental samples.

The theory of ceramic materials and their reactions one with another is best regarded as an essential tool in resolving problems or refining results. Without it, progress is very slow and will depend entirely upon the amount of experience accumulated. An understanding of the basic theoretical possibilities and techniques can help to resolve difficulties by indicating the path or paths which may lead to a satisfactory or even elegant solution.

11 Glaze preparation and application

Glaze making requires an understanding of the theory of ceramic materials, the ability to extract useful information from published experimental data and practical experiments. This chapter deals with the preparation of glaze materials as well as methods of direct glazing using materials such as ash and salt.

Theoretical information is a useful guide, but is often too refined to be used without further experiments. When an interesting line of investigation is found, it should be seen as a starting point.

It is usually convenient to have most of one's glazes maturing at the same temperature so that a variety can be done in one firing.

It is a tradition that stoneware glazes mature between 1250°C and 1280°C, but a rich and varied range of glazes could be developed, which mature at 1200°C with a consequent reduction in firing costs.

There is no substitute for trials and experiments. Published recipes reveal only that someone obtained a good result using the recipe in their kiln, with their versions of the materials detailed over a firing cycle not usually specified. When making experiments a satisfactory result may be obtained, but it should be realized that this is a matter of chance. Apart from the limit formulae described in the previous chapter there are certain classic stoneware glaze recipes which can be used as the basis for glazes. These can be varied in colour and texture by the addition of colouring oxides and clays.

Feldspar	40	70	40	25
Quartz	30			
Whiting	20	15		
Clay	10	15	20	25
Ash			40	50

These glazes which mature normally between 1250°C–1280°C will vary according to the type of feldspar used. The clay usually used in such recipes is china clay but interesting results can be revealed by using other types of stoneware clays. *Pottery and Ceramics* includes a list of glaze materials and their possible uses as do some of the books listed under further reading.

When trial recipes are recorded, a note of the suppliers and code references for the materials used should be kept. If working from a molecular formula one must have an analysis of each material to be used.

When the theoretical glaze has been composed and written as a batch or percentage recipe, the materials must be prepared so that they are in a safe and convenient form. Toxic or soluble materials must be fritted so

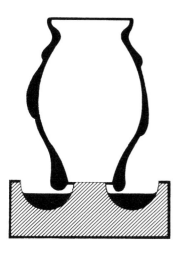

78 A section through a pot and support designed to hold the pot if a very liquid glaze is in use. The base of the finished pot can be easily ground flat

that they are safe and insoluble athough this is not usually a problem in stoneware glazes as most of the ingredients are found in the form of natural minerals which will melt at stoneware temperatures.

Earthenware glazes normally include some fritted material as the two major fluxes, i.e. lead and alkaline compounds, are unsuitable for use without modification because lead compounds are all toxic in varying degrees and alkaline compounds are soluble in water. These materials are normally fritted with silica by heating the appropriate quantities in a fritting furnace until they are melted and then poured into water to cool the liquid glass. The glass breaks up on rapid cooling and can be ball milled to reduce it to a particle size where all the material will pass through a 200 mesh sieve. When fritting lead compounds toxic fumes may be given off so the process must be carried out in a well ventilated area or in an extraction booth.

All materials used in glaze recipes should normally pass through a 200 mesh sieve. If materials are used which you find for yourself it will probably be necessary to crush and ball mill these rocks or earths to ensure an even particle size. Coarse particles take longer to melt than fine materials so an uneven particle size can result in an uneven melt. This may prove very attractive but only tests will reveal whether this is so.

The prepared ingredients are weighed out and mixed in water to the consistency of cream and then this suspension is put through a 200 mesh sieve. The exact proportion of water to solid material depends upon the porosity of the ware (raw or bisquited) and hence the 'take up' when the ware is dipped or poured with glaze. Once satisfactory consistency has been found the pint weight should be measured and noted. Future batches may then be made up to the same consistency with the assurance that it will provide a suitable deposit of glaze on ware made from the same clay and fired to the same bisquit temperature.

Because stoneware and porcelain are fired to relatively high temperatures glazes can be made from naturally occurring minerals which are insoluble and non-toxic. To test materials in fixed proportions a binary or triaxial system can be used. If a glass making material and a fluxing material are selected a glaze will be formed if the mixture is fired to a high enough temperature or a proportional mix is arrived at that will melt at the temperature desired for firing. As feldspars are naturally occurring minerals that combine glass making and fluxing elements, and often require only minor additions to produce a satisfactory glaze when fired to 1250°C+, they tend to feature in most stoneware glazes. Feldspar is also not expensive. Deposits are found throughout the world, although the composition can vary a lot from one deposit to another.

In most colleges and many studios it is common practice to fire ware twice. The first firing is a bisquit firing to convert the clay to ceramic which makes it safer to handle. In the case of bone china, soft paste porcelain and earthenware, it is essential because the glaze firing is lower than the maturing temperature of the body. After the first firing the glaze is applied and the ware fired again to mature the glaze.

Raw glazing

Once firing is more economical in time and energy, providing the loss rate or the proportion of 'seconds' does not erode this advantage. Salt glazing is normally carried out as a once firing process although bisquit ware is used by some potters. This topic is discussed elsewhere (see page 138). There is no reason why ware should not be once fired provided that appropriate raw glazes are developed and applied at a suitable consistency for the type of ware made. Robust pots with strong lips and spouts will accept quite a thick deposit of glaze without being damaged. Thinner pots with finer details will require a lighter layer of glaze. The problem is that the unfired clay absorbs water and expands when glaze suspended in water is applied. Two faults can occur. The pot may be weakened by the absorption of water to the point where it deforms, cracks or collapses, or when applying glaze to a leather hard or dried pot the water will expand the interior surface to the point where it cracks the unglazed outer surface.

Glazes which are to be applied to unfired clay ware must be composed so that they will dry and shrink before and during the firing at the same rate as the clay ware. Failure to do this will result in the glaze shelling off the pot in the early stages of firing and the evidence of this will be patches or pools of glaze on the kiln shelves when the kiln is opened. To achieve the match between glaze and clay shrinkage plastic clay is a fundamental element in a once fired glaze composition. A flux is also required, which would be a feldspar in the case of stoneware glaze, perhaps supplemented with whiting, talc or other secondary fluxes. The proportion of clay to flux may be as high as 50/50 or as low as 25/60 with some silica in the form of flint or quartz to increase the glass forming material. Ball clay is commonly used as the clay ingredient, but bentonite (up to 5 per cent) may be used in low clay recipes. Sometimes a stoneware glaze formulated to fit bisquited ware can be converted to a raw glaze simply by adding bentonite.

Some types of ware, plates or pots with substantial shoulders, can be simply dusted with powdered glaze or ash, but if the glaze contains silica it is unsafe for dusting because some of the silica may be breathed in. Clay dust also is harmful so dusting is most suitable for ash, when the results can be similar to those achieved in a wood fired kiln where the ash is carried on to the ware during firing and forms a glaze where it settles.

The ash must be prepared for dusting as described in Appendix 3 and sieved wet through an 80 mesh sieve. The ash passing through is then dried by heating it on top of a kiln or in a drier. When dry it is put into the 80 mesh sieve which is held over the pot and shaken gently. The thickness of deposit is a matter of preference, but when sufficient has been applied the ware is lifted gently on to a kiln shelf. Do not dust ash on to the pot whilst it is on the kiln shelf, because some will fall upon the shelf and form a glaze when the shelf is fired in the kiln. The dust does not adhere to the pot until it fuses so if the pot is carelessly handled some of the deposit of ash will be dislodged. Similarly, if the kiln forces flames or gases over the pot some of the ash may be dislodged to leave a thin deposit on the pot and an unwanted deposit upon either the kiln shelf or adjacent pots. You can put the pot in a saggar for protection.

The technique of dusting is very effective when carried out over a pot which has previously been glazed with a normal raw glaze. Do not overdo the ash dusting as it will lower the maturing temperature of the glaze. Try it first on matt or dry glazes, or if you have an ash which gives a dry result on its own, try it on a plate or the inside of a bowl glazed with a soft or glossy glaze. When trying these combinations assume that a eutectic may be formed and set the pot so that if the glaze does run off the pot it can be caught in a bowl rather than damage the kiln shelf.

Dusting can be carried out on leather hard pots or on those which are bone dry. If the inside of the pot is to be glazed then raw glaze it as described below before dusting the rest of it.

Raw glaze can be applied either to leather hard pots in which case a high clay recipe should be used or on bone hard pots when a recipe with less clay is appropriate. Leather hard pots should be given a quite heavy, creamy layer of glaze and the interiors can be glazed before handles or spouts are added and while the pots are still on the wheel before they are turned. The outside can be glazed only when the pot is otherwise complete. The glaze may be poured, sprayed or dipped on to the pot, but in each case it should be dried quickly to restrict the penetration of water into the clay. Handles can be difficult if a thick deposit of glaze is required. All the surfaces of the handle become coated and the water will weaken the structure of a dried handle. It is safer to glaze such ware when it is leather hard and set it to dry with the handle facing the source of heat, but not too near or the handle will dry faster than the rest of the pot and crack away from it.

The thickness of glaze deposited upon dipped ware can be modified by thinning the glaze with water. Plastic clay in the glaze will hold water so the less glaze on the surface of the pot the quicker it will dry. When a thinner deposit of glaze has dried to a leather hard state or slightly drier the pot can be dipped again in the glaze and dried.

The process of raw glazing lends itself most readily to robust forms where the thickness of details is sufficient to withstand the softening effect of water penetration. Thinner walled pots require more careful control of the glaze deposit and even when they withstand the initial glazing process the glaze may soften the body at stoneware temperatures so that the pot distorts or collapses during firing.

The successful use of raw glazing can lead to a reappraisal of techniques of decoration or a new awareness of the relationship between clay and glaze which are similar in composition and physical characteristics.

12 Other forms of decoration

Decoration of any pottery is one of the fundamental aesthetic issues for a potter or designer. Sometimes the ware is complete without even a glaze, at other times an elaborate and complex range of techniques may be called for. The richness and variety which is possible is only matched by the diversity of opinion regarding what is right for a particular object. There is a tendency for the relatively inexperienced to plunge into ever increasing sophisticated techniques of decoration, but many of the most valued pots are remarkable for their restraint, simplicity and invention within quite simple processes and tools. Mechanical application of decoration is often technically complex, but tends towards relatively bland visual qualities. Hand decoration is usually modest in technique, but at best establishes very subtle relationships between the different parts of the decoration and the overall design when applied to a handmade form.

In industry, the design of the shape of the pots and the design of the pattern which is applied to the shape are seen as two related but separate issues. Most manufacturers hope to make a shape which will carry several different designs thereby extending the range of wares which can be marketed. Many studio potters will make a standard range of ware but by the very processes they use tend away from industrial repetition. Form and decoration are seen as more unified and are usually made by the same person. Sometimes a pot will be made in a particular way or from a particular material which will contribute to a chosen decorative quality.

The designer looks for a form which will be fully developed before it is produced in quantity and designs it in such a way that the objectives can be communicated to the people who will be involved in manufacturing it. Throughout the process of making and finishing a good potter is in a state of continuous dialogue with the form of the pot, the materials and techniques from which it is made and the decoration, if any, which is added to it.

Decoration during forming — colour and texture

The choice of clay or clays used to make the pot can produce decorative qualities which are sufficient in themselves. Coloured clays, naturally occurring, if they are compatible, i.e. will not crack apart during drying and firing, can be used to produce agate ware but it is usually necessary to select a single clay or body and modify some of it by the addition of colouring agents, either oxides or commercial body stains.

Clays selected for their iron content can produce iron spots which burn through light coloured glazes particularly under reduction firing

79 Glazed agate. Ming dynasty, 16th–17th century. Gulbenkian Museum, Durham

conditions. Stamped or applied (sprigged) details on the form will be enhanced by glazes which produce different reactions according to the final thickness when fired. So by careful selection of clay and glaze a variety of glaze reactions can be encouraged.

A fundamental feature of the decoration of stoneware and porcelain is the traditionally limited palette of colour. Until fairly recently, there were few commercial colours which would withstand firing to 1200°C+ without some volatilization. The temperature was simply too high and the elements producing colour would dissociate from the clay and glaze, escaping with the heat and gases from the kiln. The traditional cobalt blue decoration on hard paste porcelain fired to 1400°C was inevitable because cobalt was the only oxide which could withstand these temperatures. Colours in stoneware tend to be limited within a range of buff, brown, red/brown, orange, purple/brown, black and white, and to European eyes these have been seen as sombre and dull. Since about 1950 subtle qualities of colour and texture and quietude have come to be appreciated by an increasing number of people in the West and if anything the scale has tipped rather too far towards the muted palette.

A natural product of these limitations was and still is the development of a variety of techniques to enrich the clay and glaze reactions and is a particularly fruitful area for experiments to develop individual appreciation of the qualities of clay. (Experiments with glazes are described in Chapter 10.) The influence of the characteristics of clay at high temperature upon the glaze is considerable and however the clay or only the surface of the clay is changed, it will almost certainly influence the quality even of opaque glazes.

80 Water dropper in the form of a duck, celadon glaze. National Museum of Korea

Another characteristic of stoneware is a concentration on texture in clay and glaze: apparent spontaneity and ease of gesture, the qualities of the natural world, pebbles, water, sand, rock structure and texture and the sky are associations which both potters and collectors appreciate, which is why open flame firing is a vital feature of the work of many stoneware potters. The lick of flames across one side of the pot, the accidental deposit of wood ash upon a glaze, the migration of metal oxides from one pot to another are valued attributes of the open firing process, so much so that they are often contrived; for example, copper oxide, which will volatilize at a high temperature, thrown into the fire box or painted upon a nearby kiln prop. The higher the temperature, the greater the reaction is a widely held belief and is a pitfall for the inexperienced potter. Attempting to 'roast' a pot can, and often does, result in deformation of the clay causing bloating or the collapse of the form.

Decorative qualities in stoneware and porcelain clays

The temperature to which stoneware clays are fired is sufficient to vitrify the clay and promote reactions between clay and glaze which are unique. Iron in the body will often melt into the glaze and produce spots of brown colour with haloes of different colour according to the elements within the glaze. Coarse inclusions of feldspar on the body may fuse and flux the glaze in surrounding areas producing runs which vary in length according to, a) the amount of feldspar in the area, b) the form of the pot and especially the form in the area of the inclusion, c) the temperature to

81 Dish with metalled rim, Ting ware. Sung dynasty (960–1279). Percival David Foundation of Chinese Art, London

which the piece is fired, and d) the time during which the pot remains at or above this temperature.

Whilst feldspar is given as an example of an inclusion designed to influence the quality of the glazed surface experiment may be made with almost any materials. Naturally, those materials which flux without volatilizing at the temperature to which the work is fired, will produce soft or funning areas of glaze. If these inclusions are coloured with small amounts of colouring oxides the spots or runs will be coloured, probably taking the form of coloured rings in the case of spots and streaks of colour where the glaze runs. Eutectics may be formed by the fluxing inclusion and the glaze, so it is advisable to take precautions to prevent the glaze running on to the kiln shelf and fastening the pot to it. Consult the appendix on page 148 for a list of fluxes, all of which can be tested separately and in combination. The more numerous the materials associated to form inclusion, the more likely the possibility of a eutectic reaction and the more fluid may be the reaction.

Refractory materials may be added to the clay, the most common being grog, sand or coarse quartz. This has the effect of increasing the thermal expansion of the body which may be desirable if the glaze to be applied tends to craze. If excessive amounts are added, the glaze may peel

82 Celadon stem cup. Early T'ang (618–907) or Sui (581–618).

(page 106) or the pot may dunt. Sand is often added, not to produce a visual or tactile variation in the finished piece, but to change an otherwise smooth clay by opening it (increasing the size of pores) and giving 'bite' to the clay so that it feels less slippery or greasy during forming, particularly when throwing.

Coloured grog may be added to the clay and this is made by adding colouring oxides to raw clay which is then fired, crushed and milled to produce the desired particle size. The results can be passed through graded vibratory sieves to separate the particles by size. From these various grades you can select the size or sizes of inclusion you wish to use.

Vegetable matter may be added to the clay before forming and will burn out in the early stages of firing to leave a residual ash which can affect the glaze by acting as a flux, with or without colour, or it may be refractory and matt the glaze in those areas in which the inclusion comes into contact with the glaze. The addition of vegetable matter will leave cavities within the clay when it burns away and sawdust is often used to produce the same effect, also reducing the weight of the finished pot.

When firing clay with vegetable matter inclusion adequate ventilation of the kiln should be ensured during the early stages (say up to 950°C). If necessary hold the kiln at a heat below the sintering temperature and ventilate thoroughly so that the body will not contain trapped gas, thus causing bloating at a later stage in the firing (see page 135).

Including otherwise foreign materials into the clay will affect the homogeneity of the clay striven for in preparing the raw clay and improving its workability. It makes sense to look for relatively unrefined clay if there is interest in achieving the qualities produced from the above suggestions.

Alternatively, the inclusion can be applied solely to the surface of the finished pot, and this should be done whilst the clay is still relatively soft. If the form permits it can be rolled in a bed of the inclusion material. If the resultant particles project too far above the surface of the clay form they can be pressed down with a soft leather or rubber pad. If the pot cannot be rolled in the material it can be sprinkled over the form and pressed home. As described on page 110, wood ash can be applied in this manner. Work in a well ventilated room when dusting a pot and wear a mask to avoid breathing in the dust which may be harmful.

New techniques are being developed with the intention of increasing the range of colours which will withstand high temperatures. One of the most interesting is the encapsulation of colour in refractory glass beads, which will be very small and behave like a powder. When development is complete the beads are intended to withstand being fired in glazes, i.e. they will not melt, and colours which previously volatilized or evaporated will be trapped in a transparent envelope which will be suspended in the glaze or attached to the clay. It is not known when the beads will be commercially available and only time can tell if they will be used outside the industry. Potters and collectors may prefer the challenge and variety of the familiar but unpredictable natural materials.

Relief decoration

Stoneware and procelain lend themselves to decoration in relief because the glaze and body reactions are very rich and varied. Many glazes will change colour or texture according to the thickness. Glazes evenly applied will tend to run thin on edges of the form or decorative relief

83 Saggars used to contain or protect ware during firing

such as a sprig. When the glaze begins to melt and behave as a liquid its natural viscosity and surface tension makes it withdraw from any sharp edges. If the stoneware body is very coarse the larger refractory particles will not consolidate with the rest of the clay but remain as small projections in the surface of the clay body. This can produce a mottled or grainy glaze quality because the glaze in its liquid state tends to collect on the surface between these refractory particles. Such effects can be so pronounced that the finished pot appears to have some areas completely unglazed, and are usually where the form changes rather suddenly as in the sharp lips at the top of a pot or a rib on a handle. Handling them is unpleasant so this type of edge finish should be avoided.

Where the surface of the pot has been decorated with incised marks the qualities described above may be achieved particularly where the incision is a deep or broad gesture. Where the design is more subtle the glaze will tend to fill the lines either during application or when it reaches a liquid state. Glazes which are opaque but vary in colour according to thickness will reveal the incised marks although some of their more delicate qualities may be overwhelmed by the glaze. If the design is to be preserved in great detail then a transparent or translucent glaze would be more appropriate. Even clear glazes will tend to produce some colour change if the thickness of the finished glaze varies, and while this is an advantage if applied over incised decoration, it means that the glaze must be applied with care to avoid unwanted variation across the surface of a smooth pot.

Surface decoration

The clay body can be decorated by applying soluble salts to the surface either by painting or spraying, but other techniques of application are widely used. Straw soaked in a strong solution of brine (salt water) for several days will absorb the liquid and become saturated. If it is then tied around the pot or the pot is nested in a bed of the straw, some of the salt will migrate into the dry clay as the moisture is drawn on to it. During firing the straw will burn away and leave shadows made up of the silica and salt from the straw together with some of the trace elements which were absorbed from the ground by the straw whilst it was growing. Different plants may produce different effects as will the quantity of straw used together with the manner in which it has been tied up. Sometimes the shadow deposit is very vague whilst at other times the image upon the pot will have an almost photographic quality. Experiments will reveal some of the varieties, but the results of such firing cannot be accurately predicted.

Other forms of sodium, i.e. sodium carbonate and/or sodium bicarbonate, can be used instead of common salt (sodium chloride) with similar results. Small particles of glaze will develop because the small amounts of silica in the ash and the free silica in the clay will be fluxed by the sodium.

Grass leaves or other flexible vegetable matter may be substituted for straw and, instead of bedding or tying the straw around the pot, they can be pressed into the clay whilst it is still softer than leather hard, resulting in an impression of the material in the clay which will remain when the straw or grass has burnt away.

Stoneware pot by Tatsuzō Shimaoko, 1976

Form in bone china by Jacqueline
Poncelet, 1976

Porcelain cup, *Century*, by Tapio
Wirkkala, 1979

Soluble colouring material can be added to the sodium solution; for instance, copper sulphate will be absorbed by the straw and small amounts of copper will be deposited on to the clay to produce dark spots or green spots where there is enough glaze for the colour to develop and these will be red under reduction conditions.

A list of soluble fluxes and colouring material can be found on page 148 and these may be used singly or in combination, but trials should be made to determine the qualities because the process is subject to so much variation depending upon the type of clay, type of kiln and length of firing, solubility of fluxes and colours, condition of atmosphere inside the kiln, as well as the capacity of the vegetable material to absorb the fluxing and colouring elements, the ground in which the plants originally grew and the species of plant. Traditionally, this technique developed where the potters used local materials and clays which ensured some consistency of result. Potters using materials imported into their area may not find a similar consistency.

An appropriate use of colour absorption is on unglazed green or sometimes bisquit ware and the surface of the pot affected by the process is not glazed, but there is no reason why it should not work over a glaze, either before the glaze is fired or after firing in which case the glazed pot must be refired. Some part of the effect will be lost if the pot is treated in the ways mentioned above and refired to a high temperature, but this is likely only to be the carbon which penetrates the clay as it does in raku or sawdust firing. The flux and colouring elements may volatilize to some extent but are unlikely to disappear altogether.

Decoration during throwing and turning

During the throwing process the form can be changed to create a faceted one. The pot should be thrown about one inch thick and then the outer surface sliced downwards to produce facets. The pot is then rethrown from the inside only to increase the diameter and soften the harshness of the cut clay. Sandy open clay is best for this because it becomes soft during throwing and will stretch without too much surface cracking.

When the pot is almost complete it can be decorated with combs either as the pot revolves or whilst it is still. In this soft state the combed clay is soft and generous in quality rather than crisp and precise. Smoother clay can be decorated by pressing strips or coils of coloured clay on to the surface and the clay rethrown to integrate the coils of clay into the body of the pot. The surface will be mixed after throwing and it will be necessary to pare off with a turning tool to reveal the inset coloured clay.

When the pot is leather hard it can be decorated before and during turning. If the pot is coated with slip of a contrasting colour on the outside, and the chattering tool used, it will chip away slices of slip and then bounce over the adjacent area. This is repeated over the surface of the pot and horizontal strips of this chattering will cover the pot. Alternatively, the pot can be turned and chattered, then coated with slip and turned again with an ordinary turning tool to leave the slip inlaid into only the chattered depressions.

If slip is brushed on to the surface of the pot with a coarse brush the resulting painted surface can on its own enhance the form of the pot or be used as a ground for further decoration. If the interior of a bowl is to be

84 Wire cutting a cylinder before shaping into a jar

85 Shaping the jar by throwing the interior only

86 The finished jar—side view

87 The finished jar from above

88 Patting a cylinder into a faceted bowl

89 Cutting the facet of the bowl 1

90 Cutting the facet of the bowl 2

91 Forming the rim

92 The finished bowl

slipped by pouring, it is best done before turning as the amount of slip needed will soften the bowl as the water penetrates the clay. Leave the pot to dry to leather hard and then turn it to shape. Although the conventional state for turning is leather hard, pots turned whilst still soft have a richness and clay quality which can be appealing. This can be achieved if the pot is turned immediately it has been thrown. In this state, grasses or leaves can be pressed into the clay to burn away in the kiln and only leave the impression with perhaps a little ash to affect the glaze applied before the next firing.

At the stage when the pot can be turned, it can be decorated with roulettes or roller stamps or cords. A roulette or roller stamp can be made of metal, wood, fine grained bisquited clay or plaster. The design is engraved upon the roller which is fastened to a spindle by either a nut or sprung handle. When offered up to a rotating pot the roller will impress the clay to leave a strip of pattern. A cord can be a piece of rope or plaited string, wound around a piece of dowel or a knife handle. The

93 Shaping the inside of a bowl using a rib

94 Decorating the bowl whilst still on the wheel

pot must be static, the cord placed upon it and moved by rolling the flat of the hand over it. The hand provides the force to roll the cord as well as the pressure to determine the depth of impression. Again the impression can be coloured by coating the pot with slip and then turning off the surface to reveal the impression as a coloured inlay.

When the pot is a little softer than leather hard, it can be pressed to an oval shape by using wooden bats or paddles, which can be cloth-covered or decorated with carvings. In both cases an impression of the surface of the paddle will be left upon the surface of the pot.

Rouletting produces strips of pattern, but isolated areas of pattern can be created using stamps singly or in groups.

95 Agate ware bowl by Nicholas Homoky, electrical porcelain, 1977

A pot can be thrown using a body made up of different colours. The body should be divided and each part coloured with metal oxides or body stains. According to the number of colours, the way they are set together, the exact throwing procedure and the pattern of colour, stripes will usually be revealed on the body of the pot as the surface is turned when leather hard. The most satisfying results come from a basic colour for the pot, plus only small amounts of one or two other colours thrown as simply as possible to reduce the mixing that takes place during centering and throwing. Pots made in this way need to be turned on the inside as well as the outside if the quality of the body is to be revealed. The addition of too much colour will affect the maturing temperature and range of the body, so test the body and colours intended for use for shrinkage—wet to dry to fired, to check the mechanical fit of the various coloured bodies and also the firing temperature to which they should be fired. Great care should be exercised in the choice of glaze for this type of pot. Sometimes the colour on the body will flood the glaze and other glazes may fog the pattern because the glaze is not completely transparent. It may even be best to use no glaze at all.

Painted under-glaze decoration

The colours which can be used on stoneware fall into two categories, oxides and commercial colours. The oldest type of colour is the range of metallic oxides which will withstand the firing temperature of the glaze that is applied over the colour. In most studios, they are applied raw, i.e. uncalcined. The colour is prepared by grinding in a ball mill and then adding water to a small amount of the oxide. Oxides bought commercially are normally refined and ball milled before sale. All one has to do is place a little upon a glazed tile and grind it in water with a palette knife. With this type of painting the first problem is to set down on the clay surface a weight of colour that is sufficient to develop the intensity required and yet is not so thick that the glaze becomes flooded or tends to run off it when reaching the liquid phase during firing.

One can paint either on bisquit or raw clay. If one starts painting on the clay when it is a little harder than leather hard, it will not be so porous that it draws the colour off the brush as if one were painting upon blotting paper. However, the clay is usually much darker in this state than when it is drier or bisquited and it may be found difficult at first to paint in great detail. Any colour applied to clay in this state will be only loosely attached to the clay and if handled carelessly, the colour will smudge and any residue on one's fingers will produce a coloured fingerprint on the next pot touched. When the pot has been bisquited, the colour normally sinters on to the clay and it is more resistant to being dislodged by careless handling.

If painting on bisquit ware it may be found difficult to achieve an even flow of colour because of the pulling effect of the clay upon the water on the brush. For this reason some potters dip their bisquit ware in water before painting, and then leave the pots for ten or fifteen minutes for some of the water to evaporate and the rest to distribute itself evenly throughout the clay. I have found that this always produces a soft edge to the colour—as if some of it has bled into the surrounding clay. This can be very effective for certain designs, but a sharper result can be obtained by painting with colour mixed with a little water. To this may be added a little starch or preferably golden syrup. The starch acts as a fixative and helps to hold the colour in place once it has been applied. A small amount of golden syrup will add body to the colour/water mixture and help the flow of colour when painting larger areas or thin lines. Neither of these additions should complicate the application of glaze over the colour. Alternatively, bisquit ware can be given a wash of very dilute gum arabic to produce a smooth skin when dry which can be painted with ease.

One can add fat oil to the colour and thin the mixture with turpentine. Whilst this mixture may help achieve the painted quality required, it produces a waterproof deposit of colour which will resist being covered with water suspended glaze. Decoration with this type of medium must therefore be 'hardened on' at a temperature of 600°C approximately to drive off the oils and the kiln must be well ventilated throughout the firing to allow the fumes to escape. After the colour has been hardened on, the glaze may be applied in the normal way.

Other mediums can be used for under-glaze painting and choice depends upon availability rather than the need to use a certain medium to achieve a particular quality of painting. Gum tragacanth and gum arabic

96 Large jar of Tzu-chou ware with painted decoration. Sung dynasty
(960–1279). British Museum

are water soluble and can be added to the colour by grinding them
together with a palette knife upon a glazed tile or a piece of glass set upon
a white surface so that the density of colour being mixed can easily be
seen. If the colour mixed with gum resists the glaze when it is applied, it
will be necessary to harden on the colour and reglaze it. Judicious
blending of the gum and colour let down with water should avoid the
necessity for this.

Commercial colours are now available which will withstand the firing
temperature of stoneware and soft paste porcelain. The range of possible
colours is already quite wide and grows each year as more colours,
previously difficult or impossible to attain, come on to the market.

They lend themselves to use upon light coloured bodies, particularly
porcelain, and are commonly available in the form of powders, but may
also be purchased in tubes mixed with water soluble medium so that they
can be used exactly like water colours. Under-glaze crayons as well as
felt tip pens containing under-glaze colour are available. The widest
range can be found in the powdered form, and while the tubes, crayons,

97 Mouse-coloured Shino ware. Momoyama period (1568–1600). The Seattle
Art Museum, Gift of Mrs John C. Atwood, Jr., 51.205

etc., come in a much narrower range, probably only eight or twelve
colours, and are intermixable, unlike most of the range.

One's own under-glaze colours can quite easily be made. The
ingredients of metallic oxides and fluxes are mixed in a crucible and fired
to between 1060 and 1120, and the resultant mixture is then crushed and
milled until it will all pass through a 200 sieve.

All under-glaze colours and oxides can be applied in a variety of
different ways and in combination with other decorative techniques.
They can be sprayed and printed; lines may be cut into the clay and then
washed with colour so that it builds up in the line and remains as a thin
wash; wax can be used to resist parts of the clay from the painted colour.
Indeed the choice of combination is infinite.

In-glaze decoration

As the heading suggests, the colour in this method of decoration lies
within the glaze. The glaze is applied to the pot and the desired colour is
painted upon the surface. During the painting there is a danger that some
of the glaze will be dislodged by the brush. To avoid this some gum
arabic or commercial glaze hardener should be added to a small quantity
of the glaze batch. If it is added to a large batch and this is used up very
slowly, the glaze may become smelly as the gum seems to help bacterial
growth in glazes.

98 Pottery vase by Shoji Hamada (1892–1978). Victoria and Albert Museum

Alternatively, the glaze can be fired before being decorated. The difference between in-glaze and on-glaze in this case is that the glaze is refired to its maturing temperature whereas on-glaze decoration is fired only to about 750°C−850°C. Some designs are difficult to paint on fired glaze and syrup or gum may be used to assist the flow and cover of the colour. It helps if a little of the glaze is added to the colour mixture particularly if the glaze is rather dry or matt. Without it some in-glaze decoration can look dry and crusty because the glaze does not melt sufficiently to allow the colour to drop into the glaze and become enveloped by it. Commercial in-glaze colours are available, but they are little different from under-glaze colour except that they are sometimes supplied with a flux which assists in the melt of the colour and its acceptance by the glaze when the liquid phase is achieved in the firing. It is, however, more important in large-scale manufacture than in most studio production.

As in the case of under-glaze colour, in-glaze colours can be applied with a great variety of techniques.

Other techniques for decorating ceramics are described in *Pottery and Ceramics*.

13 Packing and firing: high temperature kilns

Two principles determine systems of packing kilns:

1 Fuel is expensive and therefore the more ware that can be packed in a kiln, the more cost effective the firing will be.
2 Gases give off more heat the faster they travel past a pot. An open setting allows the gases to idle and give off less heat than if they are being accelerated through the narrow spaces between a closely set kiln.

Kiln settings

An ideal setting would include no kiln furniture as it absorbs heat without providing any benefit other than supporting the ware during firing, so many potters design ranges of pots which will stack in the kiln without the need for shelves or props or saggars. Obviously there must be some dimensional relationship so that the pots will stack lip to lip, foot to foot, or lip to foot, but the pots must be made so that they are strong enough to support each other. In tall settings, the larger pots would be at the base, with smaller pots at the top. Pots with lids are designed so that the lid can be fired in place, either the right way up or upside down, so the supporting rim on the pot and the edge of the lid is not glazed but coated with bat wash to prevent the two from sticking during firing. Firing with the lid in place has the added advantage of keeping the pot round as the top of the pot cannot be distorted into an oval. Furthermore, if the lids or pots vary in size the pairs have to be matched only once and then they are kept together.

Kiln furniture

Some kiln furniture is usually necessary in most firings and this should be made of a refractory material. Most suppliers list sillimanite shelves which will normally withstand temperatures of 1350°C unless overloade, or subjected to heavy reduction. Bending below the suggested maximum working temperatures is usually due to overloading the shelves followed by heavy reduction. The larger the surface area of the shelf the thicker it must be if it is not to crack during firing under its own weight. As such kiln furniture is expensive, it should be treated with care to avoid chipping or cracking during handling, or being rendered useless by large deposits of carelessly applied glaze.

Silicon carbide shelves are stronger than sillimanite, but are more expensive, very heavy and must be warmed slowly in the initial stages of the firing if they are not to crack due to sudden thermal shock.

Never use silicon carbide kiln furniture in an electric kiln as it will conduct electricity and this is very dangerous should the kiln door ever be opened during firing, which may be done if the raku process is used or if the kiln has to be cooled quickly.

During firing the clay becomes slightly pyroplastic and at stoneware or porcelain temperatures this softening is quite marked. For this reason all kiln shelves must be bat washed with a mixture of china clay and alumina 50/50 to prevent the feet of the pots from sticking to the shelves. The bat wash need not be very thick; enough to produce a dense white coat should be sufficient. If the glazes to be used are very soft and runny, it is best to put the pot on a piece of broken kiln shelf so that if the glaze runs off the pot it will not damage good shelves. Bat wash will crack off the kiln shelves if thickly applied or if several coats are applied. Either bat wash only one side of a kiln shelf to avoid hard bits falling on to glazed ware during firing from the underside, or set the pots on broken bits of shelf coated with bat wash, placed on clean kiln shelves.

Firing different clays

Stoneware settings may be of pre-bisquited pots which are safer to handle and set than unfired once glazed ware. In the case of the latter one must be careful not to damage the glaze surface and remember that lips, knobs and handles are in a very friable state.

Hard paste porcelain is normally bisquited before firing as it is usually finely potted which makes it difficult to raw glaze. It must be made in such a way that it will not distort or slump when in its very soft state (at the highest temperatures 1350°C+), so most porcelain is thin at the edges, but becomes thicker at the base or beneath expanding curves.

Semi-porcelain which is glazed at the highest point of its firing is similar in most respects to hard paste, except that its maturing temperature 1250°C is lower and it may resist deformation if it has a longer maturing range.

Bone china is fired to its highest temperature 1220°C during its bisquit firing. As it softens at this temperature it must be set in placing sand or alumina. Alumina is preferable as it is white and placing sand may contain elements which could discolour the bone china. Open shapes can be fired upside down in alumina or on refractory setters which will hold the pot in shape. The maturing temperature for bone china is critical and the range is short. Fire too high and the pot will distort and split, fire too low and the china will not be translucent. To be sure of getting the result you want, always set some draw trials so that they may be withdrawn as the maturing temperature is reached and one can close down the kiln when the precise point of translucency has been attained.

Parian is usually not glazed, except for an occasional very light deposition to improve the surface vitrification. Because the body vitrifies, it must be treated as though it were glazed and no piece must touch another. Again, the maturation range is small so draw trials are advisable.

Bisquit firing

Bisquit firing has a far greater effect upon the finish of a pot than most potters at first believe. Fast and somewhat careless firing may seem satisfactory in that the ware taken from the bisquit kiln may appear perfectly good. It is important to remember that during this first firing the clay is undergoing many changes and it is vital to achieve all these physical changes without creating weaknesses in the structure or undesirable characteristics in the body of the pot.

Changes in clay first firing:

Room temperature to 100°C	Mechanically held water volatilizes (shrinkage).
100°C	Water boils.
100°C – 250°C	Absorbed water given off from the interlayers of clay.
200°C – 225°C	Alpha cristobalite if present converts to beta cristobalite and expands 3%.
400°C – 600°C	Water of crystallization (chemically combined water) is given off (volatilizes). Kiln must be ventilated to release large volume of water vapour. 'Blowing' of ware may occur if this water is not drawn off slowly but allowed instead to generate pressure within the clay.
400°C – 900°C	Carbonaceous matter burns away, clay gives off CO_2 and/or CO. If this process is incomplete when the clay sinters, then bloating at this time or in future firings can occur.
425°C – 510°C	Iron pyrites (FeS_2) gives off sulphur if slowly heated and kiln ventilated.
450°C – 550°C	Kaolinite loses water of crystallization and becomes meta-kaolin.
470°C	First sign of red glow in the kiln.
500°C approx	In fast firing sulphur dioxide (SO_2), if present e.g. in magnesium sulphate ($MgSO_4$), decomposes. If clay sinters before the decomposition is complete, bloating or blistering may occur at this time or in a future firing.
573°C	Alpha quartz converts to beta quartz, 1% expansion.
600°C+	Muscovite mica if present loses water of crystallization.

780°C+	Alkalis begin to make a liquid phase with silica
800°C	By now the clay is very porous, at minimum weight, all types of water volatized.
800°C+	Sintering commences.
950°C+	Vitrification commences, primary mullite crystals start to form from decomposed days.
1000°C	Trydimite may form in very slow firings.
1100°C+	Ferric oxide decomposes and gives off gas 300 times the volume of oxide present. Bloating may occur if sintering has occurred.
1150°C+	Cristobalite starts to form from free silica, e.g. quartz which has not entered the glassy phase or converted to primary mullite. The higher the temperature or the longer the firing the more cristobalite will be formed.
1200°C-1250°C	Secondary mullite crystallizes out of the liquid phase as vitrification takes place.
1200°C-1300°C	Vitrification complete, all alumina converted to mullite or entered liquid phase.
1260°C	Magnesium (MgO) if present may combine with alumina and silica particularly in the presence of lithium or other alkalies.
1300°C	Amorphous silica remaining is converted to cristobalite.

On cooling

1300°C - 1000°C	The clay body is pyroplastic, more cristobalite may crystallize out of glassy phase during slow cooling. Rapid cooling inhibits this.
1000°C to room temp.	Body solidified.
500°C - 600°C	Most glazes still plastic or soft.
700°C - 450°C	Glaze solidifies.
650°C - 600°C	Stoneware and porcelain glazes solidify.
573°C	Beta quartz reverts to alpha quartz, 1% contraction.
500°C - 400°C	Earthenware glazes solidify.
250°C - 200°C	Beta cristobalite reverts to alpha cristobalite, 3% contraction.

Mullite aids durability and resistance to thermal shock, secondary mullite increases resistance to squatting because of the needle shape of the crystals.

When glazes have solidified they will become brittle. Too rapid passing through 573°C on cooling will set up stresses within the body which may crack some time in the future.

Gases given off can escape before the clay sinters, but if trapped in the body, they may make their way through the body or glaze to show as broken blisters or if remaining trapped may swell to show as bloating when fired higher or upon refiring. All too often bloating is attributed to overfiring. Programmes for firing are determined by experience and the search for desirable qualities of colour and glaze. Methods of firing have been described in *Pottery and Ceramics* together with descriptions of colour changes.

Temperature, heat work measurement during firing

Descriptions of pyrometers, thermometers and pyrometric cones, have been given in *Pottery and Ceramics,* but mention should be made of the use of optical pyrometers, holcroft bars and buller's rings. Holcroft 'sag' bars are similar to pyrometric cones in that they are variously composed to slump at specified temperatures according to the rate of increase of temperature within the kiln. Buller's rings are shrinkage trials, composed of refractory ceramic materials to shrink at an even rate. As they are heated they can be withdrawn from the kiln during firing, cooled and set upon the buller's ring gauge to determine the shrinkage. The ring number indicated on the scale refers to a chart which gives the pyrometric cone equivalent temperature. The advantage of buller's rings is that they indicate the amount of heat work without the necessity of assessing the likely range of the firing as is the case with pyrometric cones or bars. Only three types of ring are required for the full range of firing temperatures and for most firings the median type (natural) only is needed.

All pyrometric cones and bars will be affected by reduction and salted firings. In the former case, the cones or bars may become coated in a refractory layer of carbon so that no slumping or bending occurs but the cone melts within the refractory sheath, without appearing to do so when viewed from the kiln spy hole. In a salted firing, the cone or bars will be softened by the action of the salt so rendering them inaccurate. In both cases, a pyrometer and thermocouple or optical pyrometer are necessary to determine the firing progress. In a salt firing it is advisable to remove the thermocouple during the salting stages to preserve the refractory sheath from attack.

Using an optical (disappearing filament) pyrometer

A disappearing filament pyrometer is designed to measure the colour within a hot kiln by matching it with the colour produced in a glowing electric filament. The device is shaped as an open–ended tube with the filament half-way down so that it can be viewed against the colour of any background beyond the opposite end from the eye piece. The electric power is supplied from batteries. To improve vision and increase contrast a filter can be set in place if using the instrument when the kiln is at high temperatures.

99 Optical pyrometer, eye piece on right

The pyrometer is hand-held and directed so that the colour of the kiln via the spyhole can be seen when looking through the eye piece. The filament will appear as a shadow if no current is flowing through it. As the current is increased using the control provided, the filament glows and will become brighter with a further increase in current until it appears brighter than the background kiln colour. The current is now reduced until the filament is neither brighter nor darker than the colour of the kiln. When this point is reached the dial above the viewing tube will show the amount of current required to produce the correct brightness of the filament. This dial is calibrated to convert the current reading to the equivalent temperature in centigrade.

To achieve accurate results readings from different parts of the kiln may have to be taken, via several spyholes or one large one. The surface temperature of any visible pots can be measured .

Packing a salt glaze kiln

Follow the procedures for preparing the fuel supply to your kiln as outlined in Chapter 2. Before placing any pots in the kiln check that the external structure is sound and safe to use. If any cracks or leaking areas of kiln flue or chimney stack have been noticed and have not been repaired then this should now be done.

As salt firing tends to produce rapid corrosion of the metal structure of the kiln check that all metal fixings including tie bars are sound enough to withstand the firing. Ensure that the flue leading to the chimney and the stack itself will not leak any hydrochloric acid or chlorine gas during salting.

Examine the inside of the kiln. If washed with alumina ensure that this is not flaking off in areas where the flakes may fall upon any pots during firing. Where this is happening chip away the alumina from the brick work and repaint with alumina hydrate.

Check that the burner ports, burner boxes and bag walls are clear of debris – any debris which is salt glazed into place may be chipped out of this if it can be done without damaging the refractory surface. See that the flues are free of unwanted obstructions and that the damper is not cracked as it might disintegrate during the firing.

Inspect the kiln furniture. As all shelves must be washed with alumina to prevent or at least retard the build up of salt glaze, make sure that this wash is sound and again flaking pieces on the underside of the shelves should be removed and the exposed area of the self rewashed. Discard any cracked or badly warped shelves. Check that the bricks, props, etc. used to support the shelves are sound and well bat washed.

When preparing the pots for firing do not forget that the interior of enclosing forms will not get much salt and these should be glazed with a stoneware glaze selected to blend or contrast with the salt glaze effect. If the pots are bisquited before salt glaze firing, the glaze used on the interior may be any normal stoneware glaze, but in the case of raw or green ware, use a glaze formulated to match the ware (see *Raw glazing* page 110).

The pots may be set directly upon the prepared shelves or again small wads of alumina and china clay can be used, which allow some salt glaze to develop on the outside edge of the bottom of the pot leaving lighter 'shadows' where the wads were set.

Lids will be glazed on to the pots if fired in place which is the usual practice as it ensures a harmonious relationship of glaze quality between lid and pot as well as keeping the lid and rim of the pot in shape and matching. The inside of the lid should be glazed if necessary, but the rim of the pot and the lid should be unglazed. The lid is set on small wads of either alumina and china clay, 50/50 or clay wads well washed with alumina. These pads must be close enough to hold the lid in shape at the highest temperature. Widely spaced wads may allow the rim of the lid to sag in the unsupported areas. Check that the wads are not touching the glazed areas.

Leave more space than normal between the top of the pots on one layer and the next shelf so that the salt vapour has room to flow into the centre of each layer, 1½ or 2 ins should be sufficient. Leave a gap of at least an inch measured at the closest point between each pot.

If pyrometric cones are going to be used to monitor the early stages of the firing, set them on the appropriate level and near enough to the spy hole in the door for them to be seen. Once salting commences the cones are useless because they are affected by the salt. Beyond the first salting one must rely upon colour, and if possible a retractable thermocouple which can be inserted into the chamber after each salting has been cleared, in order to avoid or at least retard the build-up of glaze deposits upon the probe. The thermocouple probe must, of course, be linked to a galvanometer (pyrometer) for the temperature to be read.

Draw trials should be set in line in front of the bung through which they will be withdrawn. At least one for each salting and a few over will probably be needed in case some are lost in the process. Opinions vary about the usefulness of draw trials. It is argued that they tend to get salted more heavily than the pots in the early stages of the firing and thus give a false impression of the progress of the firing. Nevertheless, they do give some indication of the amount of glaze building up, and with experience it should be possible to compensate for any consistent discrepancy between the trials and the finished state of the ware. Draw trials are usually coils of the same clay as used in making the pots, coated with the same engobes applied to the pots. These coils are formed into rings with a flat base so that they will stand up in such a position that they can be hooked out with a metal pole. It is good idea to leave two or three inches clear between the draw trials and the adjacent pots to allow insertion of a metal rod into the kiln to see if it is reflected upon the surface of the pot. This appears only when the glaze has built up on the pot surface; the shinier the reflection the heavier the glaze.

When the pots, cones and draw trials are all in place close or brick up the door. Remember that the interior of the door will be subjected to salting and if the kiln interior has been washed with alumina the door should be treated in the same way.

If the door is bricked up, the position of the spy holes and draw trials hole should be checked. If the interior of the kiln is very dark, use a lighted candle to set inside the kiln so that the position of the cones and trials can be seen. Do not forget to remove the candle before completing the bricking up of the door.

Salt glaze firing

A salt glaze firing schedule will depend upon the vitrification range of the clay body. In the case of a stoneware clay which matures at 1280°C the early stages of the firing would be carried out as with any normal bisquit firing because the ware is usually set in the kiln without a first or bisquit fire. Throughout this period the aim should be to dry out the clay without distorting or cracking any ware. When the temperature reaches 1230°C the first salting takes place. The damper is closed, but not completely, and the result will be a clouding of the interior of the kiln, indicating reduction conditions and a drop in temperature which may be as much as 100°C. After several minutes the damper is opened and the temperature will rise again. This process is repeated several times and the temperature must be increased after each salting so that the kiln will reach the heat desired. At the end of the firing the kiln is cleared by opening the damper and cutting off the fuel when the atmosphere is clean. It is then clammed up to prevent cold air being sucked in and cooling the pots too rapidly, and the damper is closed or bricks removed from the chimney. The kiln is then left to cool at which time you can open up and see whether the gods have smiled upon your efforts.

The salt for salt glazing should be damp. The kind used is generally rock salt such as that which is applied in road salting in winter. Too little water will hinder the dissociation of the sodium from the chlorine and may result in the chlorine gas being given off as well as the hydrochloric acid being formed. Chlorine gas is lethal and was known as mustard gas when it was used in the first world war.

The fog emitted from the kiln is yellowish in colour and may tend to condense around the kiln site if the flue is not tall enough to emit the gases at a height of 18 or 20 feet.

The salt is thrown into the burner boxes in equal amounts per salting and the damper is partially closed to encourage the sodium to settle on the ware rather than fly into the chimney.

As sodium chloride has such unpleasant byproducts, which are prohibited in some areas, there have been attempts to find suitable alternative sources of sodium. Sodium carbonate (soda ash), sodium bicarbonate (baking soda) can be used, but other alkaline carbonates, such as lithium carbonate, potassium carbonate, calcium carbonate and borax have been tried, either singly, in combination, or in combination with sodium chloride.

No single recipe or materials has yet ousted salt as the most effective material, but combinations which can be tried and will come close to achieving the finest salt glazing qualities include:

Sodium carbonate	33%	55%		70%	50%
Sodium bicarbonate	33%		100%		50%
Sodium chloride	33%	30%			
Borax		15%		8%	8%
Potassium carbonate				14%	
Lithium carbonate				8%	

The formulation of alternatives to sodium chloride lends itself to further experiment.

When borax is used it is more effective if it is present only in the last two saltings and the temperature of the firing can be reduced. It is often better to extend the salting time when using salting recipes other than pure sodium chloride. This does not necessarily mean starting at a lower temperature, but if the time is extended too much as the clay nears its vitrification point, it may be softened which will result in distortion of the ware.

The amount of salting material will vary according to the size of kiln, the number of times the kiln has been salt fired and the amount of salt glaze built up on the interior of the kiln. As a rough guide a kiln of up to 20 cubic feet may require 20 lbs of salting material, i.e. 1 lb per cubic ft, whilst a larger kiln, say 30 cubic feet, may require only 25 lbs and a 60 cubic ft kiln, only 30 lbs, i.e. ½ lb per cubic foot. The most satisfactory amount for the kiln must be determined by trial and probably some error.

The salting material is prepared in a batch, and if several materials are included in the recipe ensure that they are well mixed. The batch is then divided into equal portions according to the number of saltings to be made during the firing. If borax is included add this to only the last two or three portions. Do not forget that the mixture should be damp, but too much water may create excessive pressure within the kiln as the water is converted into steam. Wrap each portion in strong brown paper or aluminium foil. All that is needed then is to push each package through the salting-port at the appropriate stage in the firing, although if aluminium foil is used clearing the residue out of the fire box when the kiln is cool should not be forgotten.

Colouring agents may be included in the salting material as mentioned on page 40, but as they cause stains in the interior of the kiln, which remain there for several firings, influencing the finish of the ware on each occasion, it is not advisable to use them unless you are particularly keen on the results and do not mind having several similar firings. When attempting copper-red effects there seems to be no suitable alternative to sodium chloride as the salting material.

Fuming with stannous chloride as the kiln cools from 700°C to 600°C will induce mother of pearl lustres. The amount required is very small, a few ounces only, but the fumes given off chlorine compounds, are toxic. Good ventilation should be maintained in the kiln because if the fuming is too concentrated the surface of the glazed pot will be scummed; also make sure that the fumes do not touch you and that they are not inhaled.

Salt glaze firing is essentially a creative activity. Small variations in procedure as well as the clays, engobes and salting material can produce an infinite variety of effects. It is a process which lends itself to carefully annotated experiment. Some effects are unique and exactly the same material and firing procedure may produce different ones each time they are used. So enjoy the process and delight in most if not all the results. They may not all be perfect, but they will be interesting and provoke further experiments.

14   Modifications after glaze firing

On-glaze decoration

After firing the glaze it is quite possible to add more glaze to increase the depth of the original glaze or to add another colour or texture. It is not unusual to find a matt glaze that has been reglazed in part with a shiny glaze, although this may be planned and done in one firing only.

Similarly, colour may be applied over a fired glaze and the pot refired to glost temperature to drop the colour in as in the case of an in-glaze decoration. If a fired glaze is to be reglazed it helps if the glaze is flocculated so that a heavier coating is applied when the piece is dipped. Calcium carbonate can be added to the slop glaze to make it thicker. The exact amount is not critical but 5 to 8 per cent will normally suffice.

Although the descriptions given above imply the covering of the fired glaze the same principles apply to painting decoration. It will, however, be necessary to add a painting medium to the colour. Commercial painting mediums are available or the colour can be ground into a paste using fat oil and then this paste should be thinned with pure turpentine (as opposed to turpentine substitute) to bring it to a consistency suitable for painting. When firing this type of medium the kiln should be ventilated during the early stages of the firing to allow the fumes to escape. Always ensure that the colour will withstand the firing temperature as overfired colours will be weaker than intended.

Commercial on-glaze colours, which are low firing coloured glazes as a proportion of flux is added to the recipe, are designed to provide a wide spectrum of colours which bond to the glaze at between 750°C and 850°C when fired over opaque white glaze. Most of them are normally translucent and will be influenced by any colour of the glaze. They are available in powdered form or in tubes mixed with a water soluble medium so that they may be further diluted with water to produce a suitable painting consistency. If a thicker medium is desired which bonds the colour to glaze before firing then use fat oil and powdered colour to produce a paste by grinding the colour and oil with a palette knife on a tile or glass palette. Set a piece of white paper beneath the glass so that the hue can be assessed if several colours are being mixed together. If applying colours one at a time and firing between each, do reds and orange colours last as they tend to fade with several firings.

On-glaze colour can be used to make coloured transfers by blending them in a silk screen or litho printing medium. It is available commercially blended with either of these mediums and requires only thinning to produce the appropriate consistency for printing. If the powdered colour has to be blended with the printing medium it should be done in a roller mill to ensure an even distribution of colour in the medium.

When the colour has been prepared it is laid on to the top of a prepared screen and squeegeed onto transfer paper (simplex or thermoflat) which is held in place on the printing table by means of a vacuum pump which draws through perforations on the printing surface, thus holding the paper fast and flat. The colour is allowed to dry in a drying rack and then a cover coat is applied which is printed through an open screen to cover all the printed design. If more than one colour is to be printed the cover coat is not applied until all the colours have been printed. Normally, not more than four colours are used in one transfer design because of the cost of printing.

The choice of grade of screen is critical to avoid the texture of the screen being revealed in the surface of the fired design. The transfer paper must be stored at a regulated humidity as it is absorbent and will expand as it takes up moisture: if it is stored in varying humidities the final designs when fired on the ware may vary in size.

The transfers are applied by cutting away the unprinted paper to within ¼ in. of the design. This transfer is then soaked in water until the cover coat can be slid off the paper, bringing with it the printed design. As the paper is made with a water soluble gum finish the printed design is released when soaked in water. The transfer is carefully lifted on to the pot and located in the desired position and squeegeed into place with a rubber kidney to ensure a good bond between the transfer and the glaze, and to exclude any air bubbles. The transfer is slightly elastic unless it has been printed a long time (two months or more) before application and will stretch out of shape unless care is taken.

The design is then fired to the desired temperature. If the transfer is applied over another unfired transfer and then fired, the top transfer may be frizzled by the cover coat of the first one burning through the top one and dislodging the second colour.

'Spit out' can occur in earthenware decorated with transfers and takes the form of tiny black blisters which break up the surface of the glaze. It is usually caused by water which has been absorbed into the body beneath the glaze. During firing this erupts through the glaze, but in vitrified bodies this problem should not occur. The only safe way to avoid it is to decorate all ware as soon as possible after the glaze firing.

Litho transfers are similar to silk screen transfer except that a thinner deposit of colour is printed and the colours are therefore even more translucent; they are capable of much finer detail and texture than silk screen printing.

All on-glaze colour can be over-fired by accident or design and, although the colour will not necessarily vanish, it will fade, except for black or dark colours which can be fired to 1250°C+without disappearing. The results of over-firing can be very beautiful and the resulting image is flatter and shinier than normally fired colour. On-glaze colour correctly fired lies on the glaze and the change in level can be detected if a finger is run across the glaze surface.

Sand blasting

Glazed surfaces with or without on-glaze colour can be sand blasted which has the effect of matting the glaze by pitting the surface and if continued, the glaze can be cut back until the body is revealed. In order

100 Pots by Alan Whittaker in sand blasted porcelain, 1977

to sand blast carefully regulated areas, a resist must be applied over those areas of glaze which are to be protected from the sand blasting, such as masking tape or adhesive plastic. Cover the pot with resist and cut away with a scalpel those areas to be sand blasted and remove them. Set the piece in the sand blaster and remove the glaze to the required depth. You may cut right through the body of the pot to produce a hole if desired. It is essential that the resist is firmly fixed to the pot on those areas which will be sand blasted, as, if there are any air spaces on the edges, the sand will be forced beneath the resist and the shapes will not be accurate.

Sand blasted glaze areas can be stained with on–glaze colour and the pot refired without losing either the texture of the sand blasting or sharp edge of the sand blasted area. When cutting deep incisions, the edges of the shapes may be very sharp so be careful when handling this type of ware. Sand blasting is an exciting technique for producing subtle relief decoration as well as modifying the texture and colour of fired glazes.

101 Red stoneware, cut and polished on a glass-cutter's wheel. Meissen. Victoria and Albert Museum *c.* 1720

Cutting and grinding

Glazed or unglazed ware can be remodelled by using diamond saws or carborundum cutting discs. Similarly it can be ground flat on a lapping wheel. These are really glass cutting techniques, but they have in the past been used on vitrified ceramic forms and are used in the chemical ceramic industry and electronic insulation manufacture. The process is expensive in capital equipment and outside the scope of a normal studio, but a friendly manufacturer may be found who will allow access to his equipment.

In all these processes the moving part is the cutting wheel and the ceramic piece is static. It is necessary to fabricate a jig to hold the piece being worked as there is a risk that the cutting wheels will draw the piece in the direction of the moving wheel and if you are holding the piece you may be drawn towards the cutting wheel or the piece may be whipped out of your hands with disastrous results to you or the work.

Lapping wheels are slower and it is normal to hand hold the piece being ground. Nevertheless, do not let it be pulled out of your hands or it will be thrown off the wheel and damaged.

APPENDIX 1

Stoneware and porcelain body recipes

Temp. °C.	Translucent bodies					Opaque bodies		
	1350–1400	1250–1300	1250–80	1260	1200	1200–80	1220–50	1250–80
China clay	50 47 54	40 53 53 57	25 20	25 25	47		21 20	20 25 30 25 15
Feldspar	25 25 20	25 24 25 28	50 50	☆25 ☆25 ☆30	⊕ 15	☆25	34 25	10 10 20 25 20
Quartz	25 25 25	25 21 17 15	25 25	20	38	10	20 20	10 10 15 25 40
Whiting	1							
Ball clay		10	5	1		15	25 35	+ 60 55 35 25 25
Bone ash				49 50 50				
Bentonite	3	2 5						
Nepheline syenite								
Barium sulphate						50		
	Hard porcelain	Semi porcelain		☆ Bone china	Vitreous china	Jaspar ware	Electrical porcelain	Stoneware bodies

☆ Cornish stone is usually used instead of feldspar.
  Given the choice of Feldspar's potash feldspar may be preferred.
+ These ball clays may be made up of stoneware and fireclays.
⊕ Nepheline syenite

APPENDIX 2

Soluble fluxes and colours

Borax	Calcium chloride
Lithium oxide	Barium chloride
Magnesium sulphate	Sodium chloride
Sodium bicarbonate	Sodium nitrate
Sodium carbonate	

Soluble colouring materials and colours produced

Chrome alum	green
Cobaltous sulphate	blue
Copper sulphate	green
Ferric chloride	brown
Ferrous sulphate	brown
Manganese sulphate	brown-red-purple
Nickel sulphate	green-yellow-blue
Potassium chromate	green-yellow

All soluble materials will dissolve in warm water−25°C+ more readily than in cool water. If the solution is supersaturated the soluble material will start to crystallize out of the solution as it cools. Detailed descriptions of these materials will be found in Appendix 6.

Stoneware and porcelain glaze fluxes

Barium carbonate	Illmenite
Bone Ash	Lepidolite
Boracite	Lithium carbonate
Boric oxide	Magnesium carbonate
Boro calcite	Magnesium oxide
Calcium metaborate	Nepheline syenite
Calcium carbonate	Petalite
Calcium oxide	Rutile
China stone	Sodium carbonate
Cornish stone	Sodium chloride
Dolomite	Sodium metaphosphate
Feldspar potash	Spodumene
Feldspar soda	Talc
Feldspar lime	Wollastonite

APPENDIX 3

Preparation of wood ash for use in glazes

The material to be burned should be free of earth and other foreign material. It should be set in a shallow tray surrounded by a loosely bricked wall. The wood should be dry and when lit should burn easily. Choose a windless day so that the lighter ash does not blow away. Once the fire is established it can be covered with a lid and a sheet of corrugated iron is ideal. There should be sufficient air drawn through the brick wall to maintain the fire which should burn without further attention until all the fuel is consumed. The ash can be collected when cool, taking care that the light ash is not blown away. Any large lumps which do not crumble easily should be left to burn in the next fire.

The residual ash can be sieved through a 40 mesh sieve and any pieces retained in the sieve should be crushed until they will pass through the sieve.

The sieved ash can be dusted directly on to the pots or added as a component in a glaze recipe. When ash is suspended in water some of the soluble alkalies will make a very caustic solution and it is advisable to wear rubber gloves to avoid your hands becoming red and sore with constant exposure to this caustic solution.

Ash can be washed by soaking it in water. After twenty-four hours the ash is sieved and the water discarded. In this way some of the alkaline material is dissolved and the ash is less active as a flux. If the process is repeated the ash will lose more alkalies.

When the ash has been dried it can be used in the normal way.

Torsion viscometer

A torsion viscometer is used to measure fluidity (viscosity) and thixotropy. It must first be levelled by means of the levelling screws on the base.

Fluidity is the measure by which a suspension behaves as a liquid. The greater the fluidity the more water is present in the suspension and the lighter the pint weight.

Thixotropy is a measure of the rate at which the suspension thickens as it stands, i.e. as it becomes less fluid.

The viscometer consists of a torsion wire suspended from a vertical arm. A circular flywheel is attached to the wire and to this a cylinder is fixed. The arrangement is such that the wire can revolve but in so doing it turns the flywheel and the cylinder. A beaker of slip is set so that the

102 Torsion viscometer. In use the slip container is moved so that the cylinder can rotate in the slip

103 The fly wheel and calibrated ▷ outer rim from which the overswing can be read

cylinder is immersed and the flywheel revolved through 360° and locked. The slip is stirred and the lock released so that the wire unwinds, spinnng the flywheel as it does so. As the pointer swings past zero the overswing is measured by the furthermost position to which the pointer swings. Three such readings are taken and the average overswing is a measure of the fluidity of the slip.

To measure the thixotropy the flywheel is rotated through 360° and locked. The slip is stirred and one minute allowed to elapse before a reading is taken. The difference between the reading for fluidity and the reading after one minute is the measure of the thixotropy.

When you have a slip which casts without problems measure the thixotropy, viscosity and pint weight. Future batches of slip with the same values should cast equally well.

To decrease the viscosity add more clay to the suspension.
To increase the pint weight add more clay to the suspension.
To increase the viscosity add more deflocculant.
To increase the viscosity and reduce the pint weight add more water.
To increase the thixotropy add more clay.
To decrease the thixotropy add more deflocculant.

Deflocculation curve

A deflocculation curve is used to determine the proportion of defloccu-lant required to produce the optimum casting characteristics of a clay/water slip.

The amount of water likely to be required in the finished slip must be assessed but as a guide a pint weight of 35 ozs should be aimed at for the following: bone china, stoneware clay, porcelain clay and white earthenware.

At these pint weights the clay/water suspension is not very fluid. To a chosen volume (¼ pint) add small quantities of deflocculant. The deflocculant is dissolved in a small quantity of water and this solution is put into a burette so that measured quantities can be added to the slip. The viscosity of the undeflocculated slip is measured and plotted on a graph where the amount of deflocculant is stated upon the base and the viscosity is shown on the vertical axis as degrees of overswing. A quantity of deflocculant is added and the viscosity is measured after stirring the suspension. Further additions are made and with each addition the viscosity is measured and plotted on the graph until the viscosity is no longer increased and finally begins to decrease as more deflocculant is added.

The points on the graph are linked and the resultant curve should show a plateau at the top. This indicates some tolerance of the amount of deflocculant required to achieve optimum fluidity.

Normally between 0.3 and 0.5 per cent of the dry weight of the clay in the suspension is the weight of deflocculant required to produce a good casting slip.

The experiment may be repeated using different deflocculants on different pint weights of slip. To determine the best composition the deflocculant slips should be cast in test moulds to determine the casting characteristics. Deflocculants include:

Sodium silicate
Sodium silicate and soda ash
Calgon: a commercial preparation of sodium hexametaphosphate.

Materials used in ceramics

Compound	Formula	Molecular weight	Melting point	Coefficient of expansion (10^{-6})
Albite - *see* feldspar soda			1300	
Amblygonite	$Li(FOH)AlPO_4$			
Alumina	Al_2O_3	101.9	2050	5.9
Alumina hydrate	$Al(OH)_3$	78(156)		
Aluminium hydroxide	$Al_2(OH)_6$	156		
Anorthite - *see* feldspar lime				
Antimony trioxide	Sb_2O_3	291.5	652	
" pentoxide	Sb_2O_5	323.5	930	
Ball Clay	$Al_2O_3SiO_2 2H_2O$	258		
Barium carbonate	$BaCO_3$	197.4	900	
" chloride	$BaCl_2 2H_2O$	244.3	113	
" chromate	$BaCrO_4$	253.4		
" hydroxide	$Ba(OH)_2$	171.4	408	
" oxide	BaO	153.4	1923	14
" sulphate	$BaSO_4$	233.4	1580	18.1
Bentonite − *see* Montmorillonite				
Bauxite	$Al_2O_3 2H_2O$			
Beryllium oxide	BeO	25	2530	6
Bismuth trioxide	BiO_3	466	820–860	
" subnitrate				
Bone ash	$3CaOP_2O_5$	310.2 (103)	1360	
Boracic acid	$B_2O_3 3H_2O$	123.7	184–186	
Boracite	$6MgOMgCl_2 8B_2O_3$			
Borax	$Na_2O2B_2O_3 10H_2O$	381.5	75	
Anhydrous borax	$Na_2O2B_2O_3$	201.3	741	- 0.03
Boric oxide	B_2O_3	69.6	577	
Boro calcite	$CaO2B_2O_3 6H_2O$	304		
Cadmium oxide	CaO	128.4	1426	
Calcium metaborate	$Ca(BO_2)_2$	125.7	1154	
Calcium carbonate	$CaCO_3$	100.1	825	4.4
Calcium chloride	$CaCl_2$	111	772	19.6
" fluoride	CaF_2	78.1	1360	
" hydroxide	$Ca(OH)_2$	74.1	580	
" oxide	CaO	56.1	2580	9.4
" phosphate	$Ca_3(PO_4)_2$	310.2(103)	1670	
" sulphate	$CaSO_4 2H_2O$	172.2	128	36.6
China clay	$Al_2O_3SiO_2 2H_2O$	258	1770	
China stone	$CaONa_2OK_2O3Al_2O_3 24SiO_2$			
Chromic oxide	Cr_2O_3	152	2435	
" sulphate	$Cr_2(SO_4)_3$	662.5	100	

Chrome alum	$Cr_2(SO_4)_3K_2SO_4$	238	110	
Cobaltic oxide	Co_2O_3	165.9	900	
Cobalt black	Co_3O_4	240.8	900	
Cobaltous oxide	$CaCO_3$	749	1935	
" nitrate	$Co(NO_3)_2H_2O$	291.1	55	
" sulphate	$CoSO_4 7H_2O$	281.1	420	
Cobaltous silicate	Co_2SiO_4	209.9	1345	
Colemanite	$2CaO3B_2O_35H_2O$	412(206)		
Copper carbonate	$CuCO_3$	221.2	200	
" chloride	$CuCl_2 2H_2O$	170.5	110	
" sulphate	$CuSO_4$	159.6	650	
" sulphate	$CuSO_4 5H_2O$	249.7	250	
Cornish stone	$K_2OAl_2O_38SiO_2$	678	1230	
Corundum	Al_2O_3		2650	
Cupric oxide	CuO	79.6	1326	7.3
Cuprous oxide	Cu_2O	143.1	1235	
Cryolite	$3NaFAlF_3$	210	1020	
Dolomite	$CaCO_3MaCO_3$	184.4	730-760	
Feldspar potash	$K_2OAl_2O_36SiO_2$	556.5	1250	
Feldspar soda	$Na_2OAl_2O_36SiO_2$	524.3	1100	
" lime	$CaOAl_2O_32SiO_2$	278.1	1550	
see also Spodumene and Petalite				
Ferri chloride	$FeCl_3$	162	306	
" hydroxide	$Fe(OH)_3$	106.9	500	
" oxide	Fe_2O_3	159.7	1565	8.4
" sulphate	$Fe_2(SO_4)_3$	399.9	480	
Ferrous carbonate	$FeCO_3$	115.9		
" oxide	FeO	71.9	1420	
" sulphate	$FeSO_4 7H_2O$	278.1	100	
" sulphide	FeS	87.9	1199	
Ferroso-ferric oxide	Fe_3O_4	231.6	1538	
Fireclay	$Al_2O_36SiO_2$	463.8		
Flint	SiO_2	60.1	1600-1750	
Fluorspar	CaF_2	78.1	1330	
Galena - *see* Lead sulphide				
Gold chloride	$AuCl_3$	303.6		
Gypsum	$CaSO_4 2H_2O$		150	
Haematite - *see* Ferri oxide				
Illmenite	$FeOTiO_2$	152	150	
Kaolinite	$Al_2O_32SiO_2 2H_2O$			
Lead bisilicate	$PbO2SiO_2$	343.3	815	
" metaborate	$PbOB_2O_3H_2O$	310.9	160	
" carbonate (white lead)	$PbCO_3$	267.2	315	
" chloride	$PbCl_2$	278.1	501	
" chromate	$PbCrO_4$	323.2	844	
" oxide	PbO	223.2	888	10.6
(red lead)	Pb_3O_4	685.6	500	
" silicate	$PbSiO_2$	283.3	766	
" sulphide	PbS	239	1114	
Lepidolite	$(LiKNa)_2(FOH)_2Al_2O_3/SiO_2$			
Lithium carbonate	Li_2CO_3	73.9	723	
Lithium oxide	Li_2O	29.9	1000	6.7

Magnesium				
carbonate	$MgCO_3$	84.3	505	
" chloride	$MgCl_26H_2O$	203.4	117	
" hydroxide	$Mg(OH)_2$	58.3	350	
" oxide	MgO	40.3	2800	9.7
" sulphate	$MgSO_4H_2O$	138.4		
Manganese				
carbonate	$MnCO_3$	114.9		0.2
" oxide	MnO	70.9	1650	
" dioxide	MnO_2	86.9	535	
Manganese sulphate	$MnSO_4H_2O$	223.1	450	
Magnesite - *see*				
Magnesium carbonate				
Magnetite	$FeOFe_2O_3$		1597	
Meerschaum	$2MgO3SiO_22H_2O$	297.5 (148.7)	1990	
Mica	$K_2O3Al_2O_36SiO_22H_2O$			
Montmorillonite	$MgOAl_2O_35SiO_2+H_2O$		875	
Nepheline syenite	$K_2O_3Na_2O4Al_2O_38SiO_2$		1168	
Nickelous oxide	NiO	74.7	1990	
Nickelic oxide	Ni_2O_3	165.4(88)	1780	
Nickel sulphate	$NiSO_4$	154.7	848	
Orthoclase - *see*				
Feldspar potash				
Petalite	$Li_2OAl_2O_38SiO_2$	612		
Plaster of Paris	$CaSO_4\frac{1}{2}H_2O$	145.2	163	
Potassium				
carbonate	K_2CO_3	138.2	896	
" chromate	$K_2Cr_2O_4$	194.2	968	
" dichromate	$K_2Cr_2O_7$	294.2	500	
" nitrate	KNO_3	101.1(202)	400	66
" oxide	K_2O	94.2	350	39
" permanganate	$KMnO_4$	158	240	
Rock salt - *see*				
Sodium chloride				
Rutile	TiO_2		1825	
Silicon carbide	SiC	40.3	1713	
Silica	SiO_2	60.1	1620	0.55
Sillimanite	$Al_2O_3SiO_2$		1345	
Sodium biborate	$Na_2O2B_2O_310H_2O$	381.5	200	
" bicarbonate	Na_2HCO_3	84	270	
" carbonate	Na_2CO_3	106	852	
" chloride	$NaCl$	58.5(117)	800	40.1
" nitrate	$NaNO_3$	85(170)	380	44.8
" oxide	Na_2O	62	1275	41.6
" metaphosphate	$NaPO_3$	102(204)	628	
" metasilicate	$NaSiO_3$	122	1088	
" sulphate	$NaSO_410H_2O$	322.3	100	
Spodumene	$Li_2OAl_2O_34SiO_2$	373	1380	2.9
Stannic oxide	SnO_2	150.7	1127	
Stannous oxide	SnO	134.7	950	
Strontium				
carbonate	$SrCO_3$	147.6	1350	
" oxide	SrO	103.6	2430	
" sulphate	$SrSO_4$	183.7	1605	
Talc	$3MgO4SiO_2H_2O$	380(127)	500	
Titanium oxide	TiO_2	79.9	1560	7.4

Vanadium pentoxide	V_2O_5	181.9	690	
Vermiculite	$3MgO(FeAl)_2O_3SiO_2$			
Wollastonite	$CaOSiO_2$	116	1540	
Zinc carbonate	$ZnCo_3$	125.4	300	
" oxide	ZnO	81.4	1975	7.0
Zirconium oxide	ZrO_2	123.2	2700	4.2
" silicate	ZrO_2SiO_2	183.3	2550	3.1

Figures in brackets refer to the figures by which the molecular equivalent must be multiplied to produce a single unit of the desired oxide.

The fired formula of some materials, particularly those combined with carbon, fluoride and sulphur, will differ from the unfired formula given above because these elements are dissociated and given off as gas during firing.

Conversion table for pyrometric cones and rings

°C	°F	Seger cones	Orton cones	Buller's rings (natural)
600	1112	022	—	—
605	1121	—	022	—
615	1139	—	021	—
650	1202	021	020	—
660	1220	—	019	—
670	1238	020	—	—
690	1274	019	—	—
700	1292	—	—	—
710	1310	018	—	—
720	1328	—	018	—
730	1346	017	—	—
750	1382	016	—	—
760	1400	—	—	—
770	1418	—	017	—
790	1454	015a	—	—
795	1463	—	016	—
805	1481	—	015	—
810	1490	—	—	—
815	1499	014a	—	—
830	1526	—	014	—
835	1535	013a	—	—
840	1544	—	—	—
855	1571	012a	—	—
860	1580	—	013	—
875	1607	—	012	—
880	1616	011a	—	—
890	1634	—	—	—
895	1643	—	010	—
900	1652	010a	—	—
905	1661	—	011	—
920	1688	09a	—	—
930	1706	—	09	—
935	1715	—	—	—

940	1724	08a	—	—
950	1742	—	—	—
960	1760	07a	—	—
970	1778	—	—	1
980	1796	06a	—	2
985	1805	—	—	—
990	1814	—	07	3
1000	1832	05a	—	4
1015	1859	—	06	6
1020	1868	04a	—	7
1030	1886	—	—	—
1040	1904	03a	05	10
1060	1940	02a	04	11
1065	1949	—	—	—
1080	1976	01a	—	14
1100	2012	1a	—	17
1115	2039	—	03	—
1120	2048	2a	—	20
1125	2057	—	02	—
1135	2075	—	—	—
1140	2084	3a	—	22
1145	2093	—	01	—
1200	2192	6a	—	29
1205	2201	—	5	—
1230	2246	7	6	32
1240	2264	—	—	33
1250	2282	8	7	34½
1260	2300	—	8	36½
1270	2318	—	—	38½
1275	2327	—	—	—
1280	2336	9	—	40
1285	2345	—	9	—
1300	2372	10	—	44
1305	2381	—	10	—
1320	2408	11	—	46
1325	2417	—	11	—
1335	2435	—	12	—
1350	2462	12	13	—
1380	2516	13	—	—
1400	2552	—	14	—

Orton cones are heated at 150°C/hr

APPENDIX 8

Examples of glaze conversion

MOLECULAR FORMULA TO % RECIPE

		RO₁ R₂O OXIDES			R₂O₃	RO₂				
MOLECULAR FORMULA		Na₂O .265	CaO .735		Al₂O₃ .408	SiO₂ 3·713				
MATERIALS SELECTED	OXIDES REQUIRED	Na₂O .265	CaO .735		Al₂O₃ .408	SiO₂ 3·713	MOL EQUIV × MOL WGT =		WEIGHT OF MATERIALS SELECTED	% RECIPE
SODA FELDSPAR	PROVIDES	·265			·265	1·59	·265	556·5	147·5	40
CHINA CLAY	REQUIRED		·735		·143	2·123	·143	258	36·9	10
	PROVIDES				·143	0·286				
WHITING	REQUIRED		·735			1·837	·735	100	73·5	20
	PROVIDES		·735							
QUARTZ	REQUIRED					1·837	1·837	60	110·2	30
	PROVIDES					1·837				
	REQUIRED									
	PROVIDES									
	REQUIRED									
	PROVIDES									
	REQUIRED									
	PROVIDES									

TOTAL WEIGHT OF ALL RECIPE MATERIALS	368·1
DIVIDE INDIVIDUAL MATERIAL WEIGHTS BY TOTAL WEIGHT AND MULTIPLY BY 100 FOR % RECIPE	

TEST No.   DATE

RECIPE TO MOLECULAR FORMULA

				OXIDES PROVIDED					
RECIPE MATERIALS	%	÷ MOL WGT =	MOL EQUIV	RO & R₂O				R₂O₃	RO₂
				Na₂O	CaO			Al₂O₃	SiO₂
SODA FELDSPAR	40	556·5	·0721	·0721				·0721	·4326
QUARTZ	30	60	·5						·5
WHITING	20	100	·2		·2				
CHINA CLAY	10	258	·0388					·0388	·0776
TOTAL OF EACH RO₁ R₂O OXIDE				·0721	·2				
TOTAL OF R₂O₃ OXIDES								·1109	
TOTAL OF R₂O₂ OXIDES									1·0102
DIVIDE BY THE TOTAL MOL. EQUIV. OF THE RO₁ R₂O OXIDES				·2721					
UNITY MOLECULAR FORMULA				·265	·735			·408	3·713

TEST No.   DATE

APPENDIX 9

Safety and workshop practices

EQUIPMENT

Ensure that you know how to operate safely all the equipment you intend to use. Learn how to switch off each piece of equipment in an emergency. All moving parts of each machine should be guarded wherever possible. Those parts which are electrically live must be enclosed so that you cannot receive an electric shock.

Be particularly careful when using a pug mill. Use it according to the manufacturer's instructions. Do not press the clay down on to the auger with your fingers.

Kilns should be situated in a room separate from the rest of the studio. They may be situated outside and roofed over and for a salt glaze kiln this is the only suitable arrangement. Kiln rooms must be well ventilated to ensure all the fumes produced during the firing of clay can be drawn out of the working area and that oxygen sufficient for the complete combustion of the fuels is present in the atmosphere.

KILNS

Electric kilns
Your electric kiln may be of a type which has a safety device which prevents you from opening the door with the current on. If it does not you must check that the current is off before opening the door. Never put a metal rod through the spyhole into an electric kiln.

Keep the kiln well maintained. Replace damaged elements, terminal blocks and brickwork as necessary.

Gas and open flame kilns
Ensure that the pipework is gas tight, i.e. that there are no leaks in the system. When lighting the burners ensure that the poker or taper is correctly positioned before turning on the gas or oil. If a gas burner goes out in the early stages of the firing purge the kiln with air either by use of the forced air system if available or by opening the door and leaving the gas to disperse naturally. This may take twenty minutes.

The chimney flue and any ducting should be free of leaks so that the exhaust gases are vented into the atmosphere. Never completely close the damper during firing. The resultant back pressure will force flames through the smallest crack in the structure.

Learn how to switch off the kiln in an emergency. Repair all brickwork promptly.

MATERIAL

Treat all clays, colours and ceramic minerals as toxic. Keep the studio, especially work benches, clean. Use wet processes where necessary as this will help to reduce dust levels in the studio. If possible never sieve dry materials. Store drying scrap clay in a lidded container. Avoid using flint for bat washing or other purposes where alumina or other materials can be satisfactorily used.

DUST

The dust which you can see is not the most dangerous. The finest dust is damaging because it is not expelled from the lungs once inhaled. All dust is harmful and that containing free silica especially so.

Soluble materials—some colour, barium, lead, etc. should always be used in a natural or man-made fritted form. When spraying colours or glazes do so in a suitable glazing booth or room with mechanical extraction to draw the spray away from you.

Clean your hands regularly, use barrier creams where necessary, i.e. if you get dermatitis from handling certain materials. Wear an overall and launder it once a week or more often if it becomes covered with dust or toxic materials.

Store dry materials in labelled, lidded containers.

Read the booklets *Health and Safety in Ceramics*, Institude of Ceramics, Stoke-on-Trent, and *Safety in the Operation of Ceramic Kilms*, HMSO, London.

Further reading

LEACH, Bernard, *A Potter's Book*, London 1945; Levittown, NY, 1972
PARMELEE, C.W., *Ceramic Glazes*, Chicago 1948
ROSENTHAL, E., *Pottery and Ceramics*, London 1949
LEVIN, F., MCMURDIE, H.F., and HALL, F,R., *Phase Diagrams for Ceramists*, American Ceramic Society, Columbus, Ohio 1956
SANDERS, H., *The World of Japanese Ceramics*, New York 1967; Tokyo 1967
CHARLESTON, R.J., *World Ceramics: an illustrated history*, London 1968
RADO, P., *An Introduction to the Technology of Pottery*, London 1969
RAWSON, P., *Ceramics*, London 1971
MAITLAND & SLINN, *Ceramists Handbook*, Stoke-on-Trent 1973
HAMILTON, D., *Pottery and Ceramics*, London 1974; New York 1974
GRABANIER, J., *Chinese Stoneware Glazes*, London 1975; New York 1975
HAMER, F., *The Potters Dictionary of Materials & Techniques*, London 1975; New York 1975
STARKEY, P., *Saltglaze*, London 1977
GREEN, D., *A Handbook of Pottery Glazes*, London 1979

Periodicals

American Crafts Council, *American Crafts*, New York
Crafts Council, *Crafts*, London
Ceramic Review, London
Ceramics Monthly, New York
Studio Potter, New York

Glossary

ANION   A particle which has become negatively charged because an atom has gained an electron from another atom.

ATOM   A particle composed of a nucleus of protons and neutrons around which electrons revolve. The number of the electrons and neutrons is equal and determines the type of element created by the atom.

ATOMIC WEIGHT   The weight of a single atom of an element in a scale where hydrogen is given the value 1.

BINARY BLEND   A systematic mixing of two materials usually to determine the melting point of each mix and plotting the results as a graph.

CATION   A positively charged particle created by an atom losing an electron to another atom.

CLAMMING   A process of sealing the brickwork (particularly the door) of a kiln to prevent air from entering the firing chamber or fumes escaping from it during firing.

COMPOUND   An abbreviation of 'molecular compound'.

COVALENT BOND   The bond formed by two or more atoms sharing one or more electrons in forming a compound.

DEVITRIFICATION   The formation of crystals in a liquid usually during cooling.

EDGE CHIPPING   A glaze fault caused by the glaze having too low a thermal expansion to fit the body.

ELECTRON   A negatively charged particle which revolves around the nucleus of an atom.

ELEMENT   1 One of the 114 known fundamental atomic structures which cannot be reduced to a simpler chemical identity.
2 The winding in an electric kiln which becomes hot when electricity is passed through it.

EMPIRICAL FORMULA   A formula similar to a molecular formula but which indicates the proportions of each molecule present in a compound.

FAT OIL   Turpentine in a thick viscous form.

FLUIDITY   The tendency of a liquid to flow.

HYDROSIL   A molecule of one atom of hydrogen and one of oxygen.

IONIC BOND   The bond formed between two atoms by one giving up one electron and becoming positively charged (a cation) and the other atom gaining the electron to become negatively charged (an anion).

IONIC EXCHANGE   The process whereby cations and anions are formed.

ION   One or more atoms which have become negatively or positively charged by the loss or gain of an electron.

LAPPING WHEEL   A horizontal grinding wheel used to cut or grind glass or ceramics.

MOLECULE   Two or more atoms of one or more elements bonded together to make the simplest form of a chemical compound.

MOLECULAR COMPOUND   A group of molecules of one or more elements bonded together.

MOLECULAR EQUIVALENT   In an empirical formula the proportion of a particular molecule present.

MOLECULAR FORMULA   A formula stating the exact number and type of atoms present in a single molecule of a molecular compound.

MOLECULAR WEIGHT   The sum of the weight of all the atoms present in a single molecule.

MOUSE HOLE   A narrow passage through which air is drawn into the rear of a kiln or flue.

NUCLEUS   The core of an atom i.e. the protons and neutrons.

PERIODIC TABLE   A list of all known elements in order of their atomic weights, grouped to display the similar valencies between certain groups.

PHASE DIAGRAM   A diagram which indicates the points of change of state, usually from a solid to a liquid, of one or more compounds in various combinations.

PROTON   A type of particle which together with neutrons is found in the nucleus of an atom.

PYROPLASTICITY   The characteristic of a material to become soft or plastic when heated beyond a certain temperature.

RAKU   A Japanese glaze firing technique whereby the pot is glaze fired very quickly by setting it in a pre-heated kiln until the glaze has melted and then removing it from the kiln.

REHYDRATION   The process of reabsorbtion of water particularly in a material which has been heated.

RIB   A throwing tool usually curved and made of wood, and used as a moveable template when shaping a thrown pot.

SEAM   The line on a clay cast where the clay has entered the joint between two pieces of the mould.

SETTER   A refractory form used to support or control the shape of a clay object during firing.

SHELLAC   A resin secreted by the lac insect, usually in a solvent to form a varnish.

SILLIMANITE   A refractory alumino-silicate mineral.

SPARE   That part of a clay cast produced in the moulding process but not required in the finished piece.

SPIT OUT   In clay the dislodging of a part of the surface after firing. In a glaze the production of discoloured and broken bubbles particularly after firing onglaze enamels onto earthenware glazes.

SPRIGG   A decorative detail formed by pressing clay into a mould, removing the pressing and luting it on to the pot.

SURFACE TENSION   The apparent film which covers the surface of a liquid.

THIXOTROPY   The property of a liquid to flow more easily when stirred or agitated.

TRIAXIAL BLEND   A systematic proportional blend of three compounds usually to produce a phase diagram if each blend is fired to its melting point.

VALENCY   The number of vacancies in the outer orbit of electrons, hence the unit of possible combinations with other atoms.

VENTURI   A device whereby a fast flowing gas draws into it (entrains) another gas, usually air.

VISCOSITY   The resistance to flow demonstrated by a liquid.

WET AND DRY PAPER   An abrasive paper designed to be used either dry or with water in which case the material being abraded forms a slurry which in turn fills any depressions and allows a high degree of finish to be achieved.

WREATHING   The characteristic streaks and runs on the interior of a slip cast when the slip has not drained evenly from the cast.

Index

Figures in italic refer to illustrations